Helping Children
with
Learning Disabilities

In the Home, School, Church, and Community

Helping
Children
with
Learning
Disabilities

Ruth Dinkins Rowan

Abingdon   Nashville

HELPING CHILDREN WITH LEARNING DISABILITIES

Copyright © 1977 by Abingdon

Library of Congress Cataloging in Publication Data

ROWAN, RUTH DINKINS.
  Helping children with learning disabilities.
  1. Learning Disabilities. I. Title. DNLM: 1. Education, Special. 2. Learning disorders—In infancy and childhood. LC470 R877h
LC4704.R69   371.9   76-50001

ISBN 0-687-16832-5

MANUFACTURED BY THE PARTHENON PRESS AT NASHVILLE, TENNESSEE, UNITED STATES OF AMERICA

To Jamie
Lisa, Bill,
Ruth, and Barbara
who have learned along with me

Preface

Preface

This book has been made possible because of the questions that have been asked of the author. They can all be summarized into "What can I do to help my child?" The queries came in person, by telephone, by mail.

When this last letter came, the decision was made to answer in print, to put down some of the ideas the author has gained through the years from persons who have helped answer that question for her—the doctors, the teachers, the friends, and, most of all, the children.

Dear Ruth,

Sue told me that you could help with my problem, problems, I should say. I hope so. Let me tell you about them if I may.

We have three boys who show symptoms of what we've been told is a neurological disorientation, each one differently. In an effort to find help for them we have gone to a number of specialists, each of whom has a different view. Most of our knowledge of the subject has come from reading and chance encounters with someone who gave us information.

Bart is nine and a half and in the fourth grade. He is an excellent reader now, though for a long time we wondered if he would make it. His problem lies in the area of transfering to paper what he knows. His handwriting is terrible and he leaves out punctuation and letters of words he knows well, even of his own name. His arithmetic fluctuates from *A* to *F*.

Josh is seven years old and is finishing "attending" the first grade though having achieved none of the skills. He is being promoted on the advice of the tutor whom he visits three times a week for forty-minute sessions—at seven o'clock in the morning!

My concern for him is that we've been told he has a perception problem and wonder if this can carry over into other situations so that he cannot "perceive" the consequences of his actions? For example: playing with matches and tearing toys apart. He is a hyperactive child and has never seemed to understand any measure of discipline.

I know you will think I'm crazy, but now I'm worried about our third son, Darrell, three and a half years old, who does not talk plainly. He makes sounds and uses sentences from which we usually get the meaning but understand few of the words. We've been told that he has a perception problem also.

Actually, my worry is not that he talk plainly yet but, rather, what can we do now to help him avoid school problems the older two have encountered. Can a pattern of learning be established now before a wrong approach is introduced to him?

I realize this is a long and complicated letter, but I hope you can answer soon. All three children have been credited with being "very bright," and I would like to know the best ways to help them achieve success.

Many thanks

The author wishes to thank Teresa Holloway and Esther Tallent for their help in the preparation of this manuscript.

Contents

CHAPTER I

Introduction
to Learning Disabilities

"Failing."

"Difficult."

"Won't sit still, won't listen."

"So bright but so dumb at times."

"He hates school of any kind."

"If he could just read as well as he can take apart his bicycle!"

These are expressions of dismay and hope often voiced by parents and teachers of the millions of children caught in the web of school failure, a web that entangles nearly everyone who has to work or live with such a child and his frustrations of defeat and despair.

Learning disabilities is the title more recently given a large category of problems affecting children who appear to be normal—are normal. Many of these are recognized as being very bright, but they do not learn to read or understand math or do not respond to the demands of school and other group situations.

Often, as students they have spent hours in remedial or corrective reading classes but have made little progress.

The youngsters may be very difficult to manage at home and in the community and may be a puzzle and aggravation to parents, neighbors, church-school workers, and others with whom they come into contact.

They are apt to be labeled problem children, and often punishment is used to make the child do better, usually without success.

Blame is often placed on the child or the parents. "They don't make him mind," "She isn't listening," "She doesn't try" are given as explanations of unacceptable behavior. The children have their own reactions: "I'm stupid," "Nobody likes me," "My brain doesn't work right."

Only in recent years have enough knowledge, money, and force from informed adults been combined to bring recognition that these children need more help, very special help, and guidance.

Research, which is going on all over the world, indicates that from 5 to 20 percent of the school population may have undetected disabilities serious enough to affect learning. Studies also show that more than 70 percent of juvenile delinquents have reading and related problems, and a large number of referrals to mental health clinics had troubles that started with failure in school.

There is a great deal of excitement being generated by the knowledge of what may be causing these worrisome problems, and parents are very hopeful that understanding and help are finally available. But the field is clouded with confusions in terminology and "cures." Programs and materials are being produced in great numbers—some very expensive and others not well tested. Only the informed person can select that which is best for the special and unique needs of each child.

And, while it is important to give the right educational help as early and for as long as needed, even the best remediation may not solve the child's problems at home and elsewhere.

Reading is often required in a church-school class. What of the child who cannot read? Scout leaders are sometimes driven to the point of resignation by hyperactive children. Should they be excluded? Can neighbors and relatives be helped to understand? Most of all, can parents help their children find success in spite of the problems?

This book is an attempt to answer these and many other questions and is an offer of hope to parents who perhaps have seen only the dark side of the picture. Suggestions are included for suitable activities and other ways to help the child.

Parents are cautioned not to diagnose a child as being learning disabled or to undertake a course of treatment just because their child has a few of the characteristic traits mentioned here.

All children exhibit some of these symptoms. Much of their individuality lies in these differences. Teachers, parents, and other adults must allow for a child's uniqueness and must avoid teaching and management procedures that are not suitable.

A variety of approaches and terminology are here explained to acquaint parents with the language used by specialists in various areas and to encourage full evaluation of any treatment suggested.

Most of the material in this book is drawn from the fifteen years of the author's experiences of living with children who have had learning disabilities and in teaching others who were similarly affected. Participation in numerous workshops with parents and teachers has provided unique insights into the total aspect of the problems involved.

The male pronoun *he*, used more frequently than the female counterpart, is not inappropriate here, for boys who exhibit the symptoms lumped together as learning disabilities, greatly outnumber girls who do. Case studies are used to illustrate both, however.

The dunce cap is no longer used, but the designation is still there for many of these capable but handicapped children.

Reinforced by red marks on papers, bad grades, pressures at school and home to try harder, many give up and become withdrawn and sullen or hostile and aggressive.

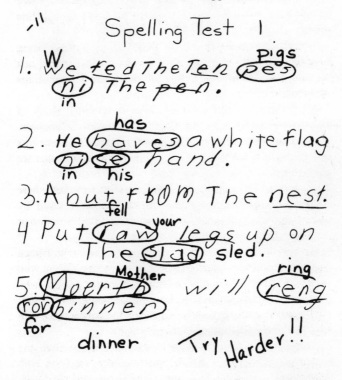

As one boy remarked, "There's no point in trying. I'm going to fail anyway."

CHAPTER II

What Is
a Learning Disability?

Shy, withdrawn Patty will not look the teacher in the eye. She doesn't mind missing playground time to correct her spelling paper, because she is so clumsy anyway. But Patty cannot explain to Mrs. Stanley why her letters are backward and out of order. She just listens and tries again; maybe Mrs. Stanley will leave her alone.

Rusty does mind missing that ball game for which he has been waiting all morning. He didn't mean to jump up and run to the door during reading time. Anyway, who wants to read that dumb book? Reading's no fun.

Rusty and Patty have learning disabilities. Symptoms they have in common are that they are both making terrible grades in school, and Mrs. Stanley thinks both are capable of doing better.

Mrs. Knowles, Patty's mother, describes Patty as being quiet and lovable, slow at some things, like tying her shoes, but fast at learning nursery rhymes and songs.

"But she's no trouble at all," exclaims Mrs. Knowles. "I don't understand why she isn't doing better in school."

Whereas, everyone knows Rusty is a problem. No wonder he can't read; he won't sit still and pay attention. His mother says, "He's always been that way. I can't make him stop long enough to do anything." The neighbors say Rusty is undisciplined.

WHAT IS A LEARNING DISABILITY?

Many disorders interfere with learning. However, the new category that has evolved to include underachievers like Rusty and Patty excludes most of the better-known handicaps.

The designation *learning disabilities* has come to mean—

1) that the child is not retarded;

2) that the learning and behavior problems are not caused by the more obvious physical handicaps;

3) that emotional disturbance is not a primary factor;

4) that cultural deprivation and environmental disadvantage are not major contributing elements.

Symptoms

If none of the usual explanations applies, what is wrong? Is this a new disease? What causes it? Unfortunately, the answers are not simple.

Learning disabilities are so diverse, taking a different course in each individual child, that consideration of some definitive characteristics may prove helpful. No child exhibits all these traits, and, conversely, the presence of only a few of these is not indicative of a learning disorder.

Very good in some skills, very low in others; good reader, poor in math; great conversationalist, can't write; good at sports, can't read.

Performs differently from day to day.

Doesn't play well with other children.

Doesn't respond to jokes.

Responds inappropriately in many situations.

Inattentive, restless, short attention span.

Cannot sit still. Disruptive in classroom and at home. Impulsive.

Unstable emotionally. Cries easily.

Excessive tiredness, difficulty in getting started on an activity.

Says one thing, means something else.

''Huh'' child—does not understand what is said.

Fights, withdraws, argues.

Difficult to discipline.

Adjusts poorly to change.

Has immature speech.

Doesn't listen; doesn't pay attention.

Can follow only one direction at a time.

Forgets easily; learns spelling words one day, cannot remember them later.

Cannot tell time.

Cannot call names of familiar persons or things.

Spells everything phonetically.

Cannot sound out words.

Scribbles handwriting that is usually unreadable.

Writes letters in wrong order—siph, ship—or reversed—dog, god.

Confuses letters that look alike—p, b, d, g.

Reads haltingly, may know larger words but not smaller ones.

Rubs eyes frequently, squints, tilts head.

Does not know left from right.

Has poor directional sense.

Can't skip or tie shoes.

Clumsy, unorganized.

Seems not to understand concepts like behind, before, many, yesterday.

Terminology

More than forty terms have been used to encompass the problems that result from a combination of several of the above attributes. A closer look at some of the terms more frequently used is necessary to help establish a common ground of communication.

Dyslexia. A Greek word meaning a reading difficulty, dyslexia is often used as a label for all learning disabilities. While reading problems do comprise the largest percentage of these problems and are perhaps the most disabling, the disabilities may be more dominant in math or writing, in memory or comprehension. The designation dyslexia might be incorrect or misleading and does not specify what kind of reading problem exists.

Perceptual Handicaps. There are many definitions of *perception,* but it is often defined as ''the ability to recognize and interpret information through the senses.'' In other words, perception enables one to make sense of what is seen, heard, felt, and so forth.

All learning disabilities are often grouped under the heading of perceptual handicaps. There is no common agreement as to which skills can be called perceptual and which belong to other processes, but it is known that perception is only the first step in the learning procedure. Such general labeling can cause undue emphasis upon the wrong process and may hinder rather than improve learning ability.

Minimal Brain Dysfunction (MBD). Minimal brain dysfunction is the technical title of the category of children discussed in this book. The U.S. Department of Health, Education and Welfare decided upon the name after research disclosed frequent use, particularly in the medical profession, of similar nomenclature.

If there is injury to the brain, the damage is so minor (minimal) as to cause only a dysfunction (inadequate or abnormal performance) in some part of the learning or motor system.

Since there is more often no evidence of any type of injury, many authorities feel the wide use of this title is misleading. It is often frightening to lay persons who do not understand its implication.

Specific Learning Disabilities (SLD). Most of the early research and application of remediation was outside the field of general education. And so the foregoing labels have not been too helpful in finding solutions. Children with specific learning disabilities exhibit gaps in learning, but not all learning is affected. They seem to be unable to acquire some specific skills as do other individuals of similar mental capacity.

Research indicates that there are certain skills or processes needed for learning. For example, a child needs to be able to discriminate visually between like and unlike shapes, to discriminate auditorily between like and unlike sounds. He must be able to associate ideas and information with related material and to remember what he is learning.

In determining why a child cannot read, it is necessary to find out which specific process needed for learning is not functioning adequately for this individual child. At the same time, it is important to know which are strongly developed in the child. Parents and teachers can then instruct the child in the way he can learn while they provide help to develop the specific areas in which he is weak.

Thus many school systems now use *specific learning disabilities* as a general classification, but they pinpoint the deficient process. By this means they avoid labeling a child with little-understood terminology.

Unfortunately, some labeling is still necessary for school boards to receive funding for special programs. Remedial programs are provided under different titles in various communities.

Causes

There are many theories as to what might lie behind these puzzling manifestations seen in so many children.

Heredity is believed by many to be responsible, at times. Often similar difficulties were present in other members of a family. As a little boy explained, "I got it from my Daddy. He had trouble learning to read, too."

Prenatal influences, difficult births, high fevers, and injuries to the head may cause slight nerve damage to the brain. These assaults are thought to alter certain learning patterns.

Delayed or uneven motor development is often credited with creating later problems in reading, writing, spelling, and the like. Much remediation is based on this theory.

Considerable attention is currently being given to nutrition and chemical factors in learning. New suppositions are being tested and presented regularly. This subject is still new and controversial.

Often, the causative factor cannot be established and may be of no more importance than discovering why a child caught a cold. The important thing is to know the problem and to treat it.

A Brief History

In order to understand the confusion and the seeming newness of the subject, a brief look at the background may be enlightening.

Before 1900 in Europe, children were described as being "word blind." The early awareness and interest in children who seemed unable to "see" words soon led to the establishment of special classes and schools.

But in the United States, even though research findings were published in the early 1900s, acceptance was slow. There was a great deal of work going on in the major fields involved—medicine, education, and psychology—but not much sharing of knowledge.

Many of the proposed theories resulted in the formation of groups to promote programs based on a particular hypothesis. But it slowly became evident that there were many parts to the puzzle and many ways of putting it together.

WHAT IS A LEARNING DISABILITY?

The formation of the national Association for Children with Learning Disabilities (ACLD) in the mid 1960s is generally credited with bringing the myriad efforts under one umbrella. A flood of public information was promulgated which resulted in the first substantial funding for special education for these children.

The ACLD is a nonprofit organization with chapters in every state. The stated purpose is to advance the education and general welfare of children of normal or potentially normal intelligence who have learning disabilities of a perceptual, conceptual, or coordinative nature.

This statement allows room for many viewpoints and encourages cooperation among the various disciplines as long as the needs of the child remain central.

These children, while having a hard time now, need not become another statistic that never made it. They could join an illustrious company of well-known persons who succeeded in spite of being hampered by limitations now being described as learning disabilities.

Leonardo da Vinci signed his name in mirror writing. Charles Dickens mentions a number of times in his writings the difficulties involved in learning to read and spell and in making sense of shapes of letters. Hans Christian Andersen was a very poor speller. Thomas Edison's mother was told that he was too dumb to benefit from school, and Albert Einstein was very late talking. Winston Churchill, Woodrow Wilson, and General Patton were reportedly all very poor students. Patton is said to have not learned to read until he was twelve years old and not well then.

"Professor Backwards" of television popularity could

talk, sing, and spell backward very rapidly. He used this to entertain.

Patty and Rusty can succeed as have hundreds of doctors, engineers, musicians, artists, politicians, mechanics—persons in all walks of life who, though learning disabled, have had understanding and help along the way.

CHAPTER III

Diagnosis,
Dilemma, Decision

Rob, a happy little redhead, did not learn to read in first grade even though a new program of perceptual training was given to the whole class.

In second grade he was given reading tests to discover on what level he could work, and a friend tutored him with little success. The youngster was not made to repeat a grade, because his knowledge of math and of the world around him indicated that a bright boy was hiding behind the failures.

When Rob's parents were told that he was just lazy and unmotivated, every device they knew was used to make him "try harder." Additional remedial work was given each year, summer school was required, punishments were administered, and rewards were promised. Rob became unhappy and a discipline problem.

He did not learn to read.

Rob did not receive help because his problems were not diagnosed properly though the parents sought help in many places. He was in the seventh grade before they stumbled upon the information that led to someone who could tell them what was wrong.

Chuck was a very hyperactive little boy and seemed well adjusted as long as he was not too confined. His mother, Sara Allen, had mentioned to the pediatrician many times that he seemed impelled to live at a rapid pace, and she wondered if there might be something wrong. The doctor suggested tranquilizers, but the medicine made Chuck worse.

So it was with great uneasiness that Sara enrolled Chuck in first grade. In no time the morning stomachaches started, and the unhappiness began to show. Mrs. Strong, his teacher, agreed that something was amiss. He couldn't sit still; he didn't fit in any of the reading groups.

So began the long journey to find out what was behind this bright child's behavior.

Mrs. Strong suggested an eye examination. The specialist revealed that Chuck's eyes were normal and recommended that he be given a psychological evaluation.

After months of waiting and with little success in school during that time, Chuck was examined by the school psychologist. The parents were then told that this obviously troubled child was emotionally disturbed and needed therapy. His diagnosis was based mostly on the bizarre drawings, the uneven scoring on the tests, and the fanciful and elaborate stories told by the child.

At the recommendation of the psychologist, Chuck was taken for further evaluation to the child guidance clinic. The psychiatrist there, after several hours with the youngster, reported that he perceived none of the disturbances indicated by the earlier testing. His only suggestion was that the whole family come in together occasionally and talk things over. The official diagnosis written in the report was "childhood adjustment."

Backed by Mrs. Strong and her own intuition, Sara kept looking around and asking questions until she found someone who could give the appropriate help. Meanwhile, a great deal of time and money had been spent and most of the important first year of learning lost.

Charlotte was not learning, and her teacher said that she did not know why; so Bill and Ann Knox, Charlotte's parents, at the suggestion of their doctor, took Charlotte to the university clinic two hundred miles from their home. After a day of tests there, including an electroencephlogram, the parents were told that there was none of the usual physical disabilities that can cause severe learning problems but that Charlotte had minimal brain dysfunction. When asked what that meant and what could be done about it, the doctor offered very little explanation, assuring Bill and Ann that Charlotte was fine but that they would have to accept the fact that she was a slow learner.

Ann cried for weeks afterward. The more Bill thought about it, the more determined he became to get some help. His search for some definitive answers led him to the local ACLD. Both parents became active in promoting public information and in encouraging the establishment of public school programs to help children like Charlotte.

These parents and dozens of others like them have gone from one expensive and frustrating experience to another searching for answers.

Fortunately, today there is less need of this lost motion because more people are informed about learning disabilities, and correct diagnosis is more readily available within the public schools. But there are still confusions of misinformation or too many choices of paths to follow. It's no wonder some parents panic or refuse to believe what's told them when seldom does anyone take the time to give full explanations.

Parents, however, must make the final decisions as to what is best for their children. A prior knowledge of the different procedures involved in arriving at a diagnosis and some of the difficulties that might arise enable a parent to make more readily the right decisions.

There are ideal situations enabling children who lack the skills necessary for reading, writing, listening, and such, to be taught these things before further progress is expected.

Most kindergarten and regular school classes, however, present materials and activities suitable to the average child. The ones who are not ready or who cannot grasp the information show up as being slow or obstinate. These unfortunate children are usually either made to repeat a grade or are passed along to catch up later. For some this works; for others, failure is added to failure, producing unhappy and frustrated children.

Somewhere along this troubled route an alert teacher or a determined parent should ask that a learning disability evaluation be made.

Clues

A child can give valuable clues about a situation, and his feelings and his views should be given first consideration. A child who expresses too much dislike of school is obviously unhappy, or one who invents ways to avoid attending school regularly could be trying to say that learning problems are present. Further information can be elicited from the student

28

to find out how he feels about himself and what he thinks is wrong.

Clusters of the symptoms listed in chapter 2 are significant. When enough of those characteristics and others noted by the teacher and parents interfere with learning, further investigation should be done.

When achievement is much below what the child is thought to be capable of doing, this should be noted as another valuable clue.

Procedures

Procedures vary from school to school. Some would require much more than is listed here, some less; others, in a different order.

1. A parent, the student, or a teacher can make a formal request, probably to the principal, for further evaluation. The clues are listed, giving the child's strengths as well as weaknesses.

2. Preliminary screening may now be done to determine the achievement levels in reading and math, auditory and visual-perceptual skills, perceptual-motor dexterity, and so on. Also, an approximate IQ score is obtained. The purpose of this is to find out if the child is retarded, is of average ability, or is perhaps even gifted. If retardation is evident, other avenues are indicated.

3. Many school systems require at this point, or even earlier in the procedure, a complete medical examination. If deficiencies are discovered—such as allergies, eye or ear malfunctions—these must be treated as part of the program or may in themselves be the root of the difficulties. If a child is

29

taking medication, this information should be part of the record. Some medications cause distorted vision, slowed responses, et cetera, and would cause test results to be different from when the medicine has not been taken.

4. If no adequate solutions have yet been found, referral is made to the school psychometrist or psychologist.

Many parents object to this part of the procedure. But *psychology* means simply a "study of the mental processes," and much time can be saved by analyzing these with certified test procedures. If an emotional disorder is present, it may show up in the tests, but equally important will be a more exact gauge of the child's potential and a charting of the differences in the individual child's abilities.

A test frequently used is the Weschler Intelligence Scale for Children (WISC), with variations for the preschool child and another for those over sixteen years of age. This device is divided into two main parts—verbal and performance—and into a number of subtests. These tests measure such things as general information, comprehension, vocabulary, arithmetic reasoning, and memory. From the total of all these parts a general IQ score is derived.

The total score is less important than the information gained from the individual tests. High scores on some parts and low scores on others indicate abilities and deficits that are important for parents and teachers to know, and these results should be included in the final report.

5. More data is usually needed to pinpoint the exact deficit so that correct remediation can be prescribed. There are many instruments available. Popular ones include the Detroit Test of Learning Aptitudes and the Illinois Test of Psycholinguistic Ability (ITPA), both divided into many subtests that

reveal such things as how well a child hears sounds and remembers them, how he organizes himself to work, how well he perceives parts of a picture as well as the whole subject, and how he expresses what he knows.

Results

When all these data are gathered, several involved persons gather to discuss what should be done. These include the classroom teacher, the person who did most of the evaluation, and any others concerned with administrative decisions. This information, then, is shared with the parents, who must decide if they will accept the recommendations.

If a special teacher, often called the SLD teacher, is available, she may be allowed to work with the child for a part of one or more days a week. The classroom instruction can be designed to include appropriate teaching methods.

When Rob was finally given proper evaluation it was discovered that he was a capable boy indeed and that his problems were mostly in the visual-perceptual area. The whole-class instruction of the first grade had not given him nearly enough practice to improve his inadequate skills. Remediation in this area enabled Rob to improve so much that his attitude was changed, and he was a much more successful student.

Chuck's main problem was diagnosed as being his hyperactivity. When proper medication was administered and both the teacher and his parents guided him in a structured routine, his learning capacity was greatly enhanced. His short attention span still made learning to read very difficult.

31

Charlotte's situation was much harder to diagnose. Her IQ potential was thought to be in the low normal range, and she had little understanding of spatial concepts. Charlotte needed a great deal of help, especially with math.

Most schools are getting away from placing these students as well as those with many other types of handicaps in self-contained classrooms isolated from other children all day. The new approach, called *mainstreaming,* advocates that children with all types of handicaps can and should be taught in the regular classroom with supportive help from specially trained teachers.

Ryon had so much trouble trying to read in his earlier years that in the sixth grade, even though there was help available, he was afraid to try until a new student was put into his class. Sandy was blind, and the very wise teacher asked Ryon to read assignments to him.

Sandy often had to urge Ryon to spell a word aloud before either could make sense of it, and they had many laughs over mistakes that each made. Both progressed, and what had been a handicap could now be talked about and even laughed at.

Sandy, of course, depended upon his hearing as a main source of strength and could warn Ryon if he heard the teacher approaching when they were not working as required. So they began calling each other "Eyes" and "Ears," affectionate nicknames that tied two buddies together in mutual understanding.

And they all learned happily ever after?

Probably not. Such complete services are not always available; the personnel may not be adequately trained; months of waiting to get on the list often lie ahead. Some children just miss getting into special programs because they are not quite "bad enough" to meet the criteria. Many

32

classroom teachers are not willing to work out the problems. Attractive-looking programs available in the community lure the parents seeking help.

The decisions are just beginning.

Evaluations and Remediation Outside the Public School

Many local mental health and Easter Seal centers offer valuable services and participate in helping parents follow through with the school.

Information is probably available at the nearest university that has an exceptional-child department in its educational training. A university medical clinic might be able to identify the source of a dysfunction and suggest local agencies to contact.

Many educational psychologists in private practice have available proper tests to make a diagnosis as to whether a child has a learning disability.

A check with the local or state ACLD can usually secure information as to what agencies or persons are available and what services to expect.

A greater problem will be to find appropriate remediation if it is not to be found within public education. The word *appropriate* must be stressed. Tutors, special programs, private schools exist in abundance, some even advertising themselves as ideal solutions for learning problems, but they may not be informed about specific learning disabilities.

Many parents immediately jump onto the idea of transferring their child to a private school, only to run into the same confusions. Smaller classes can be valuable but are not in themselves the answer; neither is individual instruction, unless the tutor is willing to go beyond traditional methods.

Mrs. Forrest, a teacher for thirty-five years and recently retired, said: "I always thought that if I could have had more time with the ones who didn't learn to read, I could have taught them. Now I'm working with a little fellow a half hour at a time, three times a week—just the two of us. And I'm not making a bit of progress with him."

Finding out what it is the child cannot do, as well as the way he can learn best, is important, no matter where or under what conditions learning is to take place.

Attractive packages by specialists in many fields beckon desperate parents looking for help or a quick cure. Any procedure that advertises itself as "the answer" and proposes the same methods for all the children who come should be suspect.

A selective parent, armed with information, will ask discerning questions. This applies to any approach whether in a doctor's office, in a school, or from learning to be gained from records, games, or other equipment. Uncorrelated emphasis upon eye exercises, motor training, or any one-sided approach can actually delay progress.

Troy was having a hard time learning to read. His teacher told Mrs. Larriman, Troy's mother, that he could learn best phonetically. Mrs. Larriman had recently read an article which stated that all children should be taught the principles of phonics. So she ordered a set of records guaranteed to teach all children to read better. Night after night Troy was made to listen to the records. His reading improved only slightly, and the overemphasis on the sound of the words

caused him to learn to spell everything as it sounded to him.
The results can be seen in the illustrations of a spelling test.

Karl, on the other hand, was slow at reading, but he was
making progress. His parents, not satisfied, transfered him to
a small private school which used only a sight-word method.

He could barely read in a first-grade reader there, and continued emphasis upon this approach did not help.

A proper diagnosis of the disabilities will determine the appropriate remediation, which probably will be a combination of several methods.

There are no quick or easy answers, and parents have to assess the alternatives carefully.

Medication and Hyperactivity

Tranquilizers are used to calm jittery nerves, and amphetamines are supposed to stimulate or pep up. But for reasons not clearly understood, many persons have opposite reactions to these medications.

It was discovered many years ago that some amphetamines and similar drugs seemed to calm hyperactive children, enabling them to concentrate and work more efficiently. The principle drawbacks were the side effects, sleeplessness and loss of appetite among them.

One of these drugs, Ritalin, has been used extensively with good results and with less upset. The dosage is so low, addiction is not likely.

Only a doctor with good input from parents and teachers can decide if a child can benefit from these drugs and other medications. A neurologist said, "If a child really needs this type of treatment, it would be as wrong to withhold it as to deprive a severe diabetic of insulin. However, it certainly is not the first avenue to take if other measures will work."

Some experts feel that medication only camouflages the

symptoms and does not get rid of the underlying cause. Others feel that the hyperactivity is the root of the problem and should be treated first.

Nutrition, Megavitamins, Hypoglycemia

The checklist in chapter 2 does not mention medical complaints such as poor eating habits, allergies, dizziness, stomachaches, and so on, because all children are subject to these maladies.

Children who have learning disabilities do seem to have more than their share of these types of ailments.

Stress increases the need for good nutrition. Children who are experiencing difficulties in school or at home are under a great deal of stress. This situation calls for an optimum diet, but often the opposite happens: the disturbances bring on stress, which in turn produces poor eating habits which may then cause the problems to be increased. An intervention is sometimes needed to break this endless cycle.

The question that is not easily answered is which must be done first—medical supervision or changes in the learning environment. Success can bring wonderful cures, but sometimes the best aid cannot get through to a child who is not feeling well.

Metabolic diseases and imbalances are known to be factors in emotional instability. There is now emphasis upon these as causative factors in defective learning. Controversies exist as to what constitutes an imbalance, how much is enough or too much of a vitamin or mineral, how rigid a diet is really helpful, and how important is the effect of food additives and other environmental factors.

A case study of a child who is being treated with megavitamins (meaning large dosage) and other measures will serve to point out the complications of such a treatment, the expense, and the results as seen by one parent.

I told you in my last letter that we had made an appointment with the doctor. We had to wait over two months, but when we finally saw him, he spent over two hours with us and with Harry.

He sent us home with sixteen prescriptions for vitamins and supplements. Our regimen at home included two allergy shots a week, plus ten pills at breakfast and ten at supper with one before breakfast and two at bedtime. Harry through all this has been a real trouper. His diet was the other thrust of the treatment. That included all foods with artificial coloring and flavoring eliminated and all foods with sugar eliminated. This meant no fruit or even prepared food with trace sugar. He drinks only bottled mineral water and V-8 juice.

By the Christmas holiday, Harry could make it through the whole day with only five milligrams of Ritalin but still had to have that in the morning. Now, though less than two months since we started all this, he is without any Ritalin at all and the teachers report he is doing his best work since October. Praise the Lord!

Of course, the expense has been tremendous and the regimen quite strenuous. But to have him off Ritalin and to have this little boy calm and reasonable and controlled is worth even more.

We realize that Harry's hyperactivity is controlled, not cured by the regimen he is on, and can be reinstated within a few days if we do not follow the diet.

Other treatments are not so elaborate nor as expensive. One approach concentrates principally upon elimination of foods that contain artificial coloring and flavorings. After following this diet for a few months, a relieved girl described herself, "Now, I'm not mean anymore."

Hypoglycemia, sometimes called "low blood sugar," is a disease thought by some to be quite rare, by others to be a contributing factor in many childhood ills as well as in learning difficulties.

The symptoms, almost too numerous to mention, include dizziness, extreme tiredness, drowsiness, insomnia, irritability, cramps and vague pains, depression, nervousness, headaches, and so on. These manifestations can be expressed, however, by anyone on an inadequate diet or under a great deal of tension.

A record of what is being eaten may reveal extreme deficiencies in diet or too large a consumption of sugar or soft drinks. A sensible adjustment of routines, balanced meals, particularly breakfast, and a lessening of tension serve to free the child to concentrate upon learning new skills.

Lay persons cannot make diagnosis of an ill or decide a need for a great amount of vitamins nor embark upon any extreme regime except under the direction of expert medical advice. Even an excess amount of vitamins can be dangerous.

Only parents can decide to whom they will listen, but care must be exercised so as not to drag an impressionable child from one doctor to another. Thorough investigation needs to be made before the child is involved.

Rob, Chuck, Charlotte, and the many other children like them can be successful if their difficulties are properly diagnosed and a three-pronged approach is utilized. For instance:

—if appropriate teaching methods are provided;

—if physical problems are controlled through medical care;

—if their environment does not allow a handicap to interfere with daily living and work.

CHAPTER IV

Parents:
The First Teachers

A child comes from and returns to the home. Outside forces—school, church, and community—help teach and shape the character of the child. But first and last, learning comes from parents and home environment. The self-concept of the members of the home is influenced by the interaction with one another.

Rarely ever are children only educationally handicapped. The disabilities that cause learning problems have been with the child all along and often have caused turmoil within the family.

Parents have learned to deal with normal situations. If an abnormal one comes along—blindness, severe illness, crippling handicaps—adjustments are made no matter how difficult.

The abnormalities that come to full bloom as learning disabilities are subtle and unexpected. Parents are unprepared to detect and manage the problems that arise. A "bad" child is threatening to a parent, and expectations that cannot be met are threatening to the child. Intense feelings of guilt frequently develop in both adult and child.

A good self-image is a determining factor in a child's success but equally important to a parent. It is embarrassing to have one's child throw a temper tantrum in the middle of the grocery store nearly every time he goes or for him to be known as the neighborhood bully. It's defeating to have teachers infer that one's child is not disciplined when a parent knows he has tried everything.

A meeting is in progress at the First Presbyterian Church. A great deal of coffee is being consumed as nine mothers and one father talk together. These ten meet once a month in what started out to be a mothers' meeting sponsored by the local ACLD chapter to share problems and insights about their children. The gathering has been so popular that a night meeting is also held so others can participate.

Marguerite is saying, "I thought things were getting better, but yesterday Cindy's teacher called and said she found Cindy hiding in the bathroom rather than going to the playground. I know others tease her because she is such a klutz, but I don't know what to do." She shrugs dispiritedly as she wonders aloud, "Go over there and see that she doesn't hide somewhere?"

Shirley comes into the room breathlessly. "I'm sorry I'm late. Mark refused to go this morning. It seems that two boys threatened to beat him up because they said he took their pencils. I had to go and explain to Mrs. Martin. I hated to leave him there," she says.

"I know what you mean," nods Eunice, sympathetically. "Sometimes I think Randy's teacher doesn't care anyway. She wrote on his report that I should *make* him learn his spelling words. I've tried, and last night I wouldn't let him watch the 'Peanuts' special because he hid his spelling book. So he just laid on his bed and stared at the ceiling. I felt terrible." She brushes her eyes as if to clear them of cobwebs as she adds, "And this morning he wouldn't speak to me while he was dressing."

Louise, lost in her own worries, continues the conversation. "Sometimes I wish I didn't have to speak to Lamar. All we do is argue and yell and then he slams out the door. He says he is going to run away and—"

"Mae did run away from school the other day," interrupts Norma. "She wet her pants when it was her turn to read, and everybody kept giggling. When the others went back to their seats, she slipped out."

Bob has been quiet all this time. It has been hard for him to share in this self-revelation, admitting failure on his part. Now he says, "I can't help wondering what we did wrong because Bobby is sometimes mean to younger children. I've caught him torturing frogs and kicking the dog. Sometimes he seems so unhappy that I ache to reach inside and help him." He leans forward dejectedly. "But I don't know how."

Finally, Teresa, the leader from the Mental Health Center, guides the discussion into responses of how to understand the unique problems a little better, helping the group to arrive at their own solutions.

No amount of perfect schooling or community support will make up for a poor situation in the home. Conversely, almost nothing can destroy a secure relationship developed there.

The child may be educationally handicapped, and that has to be dealt with, but what happens in the total environment will determine whether he becomes life-handicapped. The parents are the key.

A normal child accepts a parent's opinion of him as proof

of his worth. If a parent feels that the child is embarrassing, too much trouble, or not very smart, the child will know. Children catch feelings of those around them like they catch communicable diseases. Anxiety, worry, the desire for change are conveyed without words.

An individual has enough to worry about with his known shortcomings and inadequacies without trying to live up to unrealistic expectations.

Parents need to reevaluate their children, to look for the wonderful attributes that may be hidden, and to better understand the deficits that some may have before they decide how they will discipline and guide them.

These Talented Children

At one of the parents' meetings, Teresa asked the participants to divide a paper in half and write on one side the things their child did that annoyed them and on the other the things they did well and were pleasing. Joann, after lengthy listing on one side, could not think of anything to put in the positive list.

As she told the group later, "I left here in tears that day because I realized I wasn't even looking for good; everything was bad. So I went home and started listening and noticing." She got up to get a cup of coffee as she continues. "I discovered that Tom was fascinated with fish. He had been wanting an aquarium, but I had said he could have it when his grades improved." She looks toward Teresa. "Well, my husband and I decided to get him one now. We were amazed at his knowledge and so was the man at the shop.

"That was a month ago," Joann gestures with the spoon to emphasize. "And you won't believe the change in him—and us. We all went to Marineland, and he was our guide. He knew everything, just everything—about the smaller fish there.

"We are planning to put an old bathtub in the backyard to serve as a pond for the large goldfish. We are talking now instead of yelling," she sighs happily as she sits down. "And the best thing," she rushes on, "his teacher called the other day. She wanted to know what had happened to him; he is different even in school." Joann swallows hard as she finishes, "Oh, when I think of what we were doing to him."

Not all successes come about so rapidly, but every child, just like every human being, has a unique talent or a special interest.

—Susie had been diagnosed early as being retarded, and she could not talk, but she could hum perfect tunes, and her talent for drawing was remarkable. Her parents encouraged both. Now in her teens and after speech lessons, Susie sings and paints. She is trying to decide if she wants to be an artist or a musician. Few signs of her early problems exist. She is a bright, alert teen-ager.

—Roland could not read, and most of the school requirements were too difficult for him. But he loved geography and could draw from memory most of the countries of the world and the geographical details of each. Roland enjoyed making posters.

—Jan was painfully shy and could not understand math, but she sat for hours at the piano picking out tunes.

—Nothing was safe around Wendall because he took everything apart. In sixth grade while he was still behind in reading and no one could read his writing, he was the one everyone sought out if anything needed repair.

"I don't know what we would do without him," says his teacher. "He even repaired the clock one day while I was out of the room. I didn't know whether to scold or thank him."

(Henry Ford, reportedly a poor student, was said to be such a tinkerer that his parents had their clock embedded in the wall to keep him from taking it apart.)

—Clara was so inventive and understanding with young children that she was the favorite neighborhood babysitter. Few of the adults were aware how torturous attending school was for her.

—And so on with John and Mary, Ralph and Larry, and the many others who do not fit the mold imposed by someone else but have their own special insights and capabilities.

Most expectations of a daughter's or son's behavior come from what parents wish to happen, what they want their offspring to be rather than looking at what the child is and what he can do well.

The Developing Child

The movie *Early Recognition of Learning Disabilities* produced by the National Institute of Neurological Diseases and Stroke (see Resources) states that a small lag in kindergarten, uncorrected, may be magnified many times as the child goes through school.

Another stumbling block is that society has decreed all children shall start formal education between five and seven years of age. Many who are not ready then for the heavy emphasis upon formal learning might well be so a little later. Meanwhile they are faced with tasks which they are unable to perform, and the resulting failure interrupts what might have been a normal flow of emotional and physical development.

Parents who observe these lags can give extra attention to see that the deficiencies are improved before the demands of formal learning become too great. Some nurseries and kindergartens, increasing now in number, offer developmental programs to meet the needs of such children.

Hyperactivity. Because hyperactivity is so troublesome and disruptive for all involved, it needs to be examined closely. Probably no type of behavior drives parents ''up the wall'' as much as that of a child who is never still, impulsive to the point of destruction, a Dennis the Menace and Houdini evolved into one package. However, it is neither funny nor entertaining to the exhausted adult who has chased after this chameleon all day.

Descriptive comments include:

''He won't stay in his bed when I put him down.''

''He turns somersaults through the living room when company comes.''

''She never sits still or plays quietly. She doesn't even like to watch TV.''

''He was born that way—never lay still in his bed—and started running before he could walk steadily.''

''She climbs constantly. I'm so afraid she's going to get hurt.''

''He seems driven, can't stop himself or be quiet.''

''We can never eat a quiet meal, he's so disruptive.''

Some excessive activity is caused by too much stimulation

or as a reaction to stress, but such children can be calm at times. Others seem to be stuck in high gear and react that way most of the time.

This handicap is not the fault of the child, nor can he stop himself without help. Punishment or even rigid controls usually are of little value.

Medication may help, and a good diet is a requirement to resupply the nutrients used up by all the activity. In addition, understanding and management procedures worked out by both adult and child are essential.

Perception. So many children who later exhibit learning problems are seen first as clumsy and uncoordinated. They may exhibit poor hand control, uneven rhythm and balance—seen in skipping or riding a bicycle—and may have been late in motor development or exhibited unusual characteristics such as crawling only on one knee.

However, many of the difficulties may involve a visual perception lag. These deficiencies are usually not noticed until reading and writing are required, but they can be seen by an alert parent much earlier.

When movement and vision are combined, difficulties are noticed: constantly knocking over a full glass or missing the plate when putting food on it, running into or tripping over objects, inability to catch a ball.

Visual inefficiency—blurring or doubling—and nonalertness may be signals of perceptual problems. Thus the child does not notice changes in the environment—furniture moved, similarities and differences in objects, or errors in his work. He may have trouble staying on the line if reading. A young child may not respond to written numbers and letters even of his own name, though he may be able to say them aloud.

Auditory perception is of greater importance to the young child because learning comes through the ears before the eyes and remains the dominant force for a number of years unless the normal development is impaired.

The responses then are seen as objectionable behavior. The child who does not relate to sounds around him is said to be not listening or not minding. "I've *told* him a dozen times not to do that." He never *hears* anything I say." She acts as if she is *deaf* at times." "He won't pay *attention*."

Further indications include frequent mispronunciations and substitutions or prolonged baby talk. Sometimes the child will withdraw from too much sound or become too active. For some, attention can be given to only one sound or one instruction at the time.

Many persons can respond adequately to stimulation either verbally or visually but cannot coordinate the two. Thus a child may close his eyes in order to hear or put his hands over his ears so that he can see better.

Perceptual impairments affect other senses as well—taste, smell, touch. Sometimes these senses are overdeveloped, in some, lacking.

Whatever area of perception is affected, a weakness causes the child's world to be unstable, unpredictable, and confusing. Usually these deficiencies are not indications of immaturity which the child will outgrow. The progress made without help may be inadequate and built upon weakness. This splinter development will not allow anyone to realize his innate potential.

Research on the brain indicates that rather than change the child, the adjustment must come in methods of teaching and management. If he were born that way and maybe inherited it at that, he cannot be expected to respond as does the so-called average child. When the environment is changed, learning takes place, and even aggressive behavior is affected favorably.

Ideas to keep in mind when planning for management in the home.

1. Accept the child the way he is.

The cause of the learning problems are no more his fault than are the color of his eyes and hair, his size or sex. Some of the objectionable behaviors may be deliberate, but this is perhaps the only way he has of coping.

The expectations of the parents may have to change. Learning and behavior difficulties do not go away in a hurry. The basic cause may remain with the person always, and good management by adults involves some adjustment to the child's way of doing things.

The view of aggressive behavior and "nice" children may have to change also. Not all aggression is bad. It often leads a person into great achievements. So attempts should be made to channel the behavior properly rather than curtail the agression. This usually won't work, and the young person may be harmed in the attempt.

The neighbors or relatives or even teachers cannot be the judges of what makes a "good" or normal-acting youngster. Parents learn to accept deviations from society's approval.

The child and the parents need to assess and accept the weaknesses as well as the strong qualities of each other. A little girl, who was struggling to keep up in school, remarked, "I may be a slow learner, but I'm a good one."

2. A child cannot develop a good self-concept if his deficiencies are constantly under scrutiny and negative comments dominate his life.

William James once said that the greatest revolution in his generation was the discovery that human beings, by changing the inner attitudes of their minds, can change the outer aspects of their lives.

And so it is with children who have trouble learning some things. It is no wonder that a poor reader who is required to read much of the schoolday, perhaps attends a special reading class, is made to practice reading at home and probably to attend summer school, is uncooperative and in a bad mood much of the time.

Remediation must be tempered with more pleasurable activities, and the smallest accomplishment must be acknowledged.

Nearly everyone learns better and responds more quickly to positive statements rather than negative ones. Much management is attempted through fear of the consequences of nonlearning, with threats of punishments. "If you make any more *Fs* on your report card, you won't get to—" or "If you don't clean up your room, I'm going to—" become everyday statements with the undesirable behaviors being emphasized and the successful ones perhaps not mentioned at all.

"I like the way you put your boat on the shelf" is far more helpful than pointing out all the things left on the floor. A child often feels that "nothing I do is right." Acknowledging what is right and good without mentioning what isn't, serves as a reward because of the pleasure it gives, but it also helps a disorganized person know how to proceed.

A child with developmental patterns different from others around him needs guidance, love, and assurance of his worth, above the normal person. Often less is given because of the constant reprimands and the attention centered on the problems.

A low opinion of themselves is common to all children who are experiencing failure or who are in constant conflict with others in the family. The most important factor is to help them build a good view of their abilities. A poor attitude destroys the foundation of learning.

3. What a child doesn't know or cannot do, he must be taught if he is to learn.

Children who exhibit gaps in learning simply have not been taught these things in ways that are appropriate to them. Because they have lived as long as another or have been exposed to the same experiences does not mean that they can learn the same.

A child is not expected to mature to the skill of riding a bicycle or "catch on" simply by watching an older brother or sister. Someone usually teaches him in whatever way is required for him to learn. Neither does maturity bring to some children good listening skills or responsible behavior. They must be taught these things.

Most children who mature unevenly are disorganized and need a great deal of structure provided for them. They may not know how to straighten their room, how to start, what to do next. The same is true of homework and many other activities. They may need fixed times for meals, bed, and even free time. This routine is necessary for them to learn how to meet the demands of daily living.

A parent can discover the way a son or daughter learns best and use that approach to convey information which is not readily learned otherwise.

Some children must feel materials or take things apart in order to understand them. They seem to learn through their hands. Others learn best visually and can understand better through pictures or printed instructions, being almost unable to utilize much of what they hear. Many have to hear information in order to understand or remember.

These are not unusual traits. Everyone has his own style of learning. Many of the characteristics that come to be called learning handicaps would not have developed if more attention had been given to learning styles in early management and teaching. This becomes particularly important, however, once a child has failed to learn.

Parents are in the best position to note how their children learn. They can save themselves much grief if they take the time to teach a child to listen rather than punish him if he doesn't and learn to rely less on too much talking or yelling to get action.

It must be kept in mind that a skill has to be learned, not just shown, and ideas and information must be understood, not just talked about. Many parents become impatient because another child in the family has "caught on," forgetting that each must learn in his own way.

4. Little improvement can be made without the child's being part of the planning for change and his feelings clearly known and respected.

How a person sees/hears/feels his world determines his

reaction to it, and a parent should learn to listen and not allow preconceived notions to dominate decisions. The child will have ideas about how to solve problems that may be more suitable than anything an adult could think of. He surely will be more willing to carry out the decision if he has had a part in deciding upon it.

Adult feelings should be expressed also. At one of the group meetings Betty related an incident that had happened with her daughter, Fran.

"One day Fran was about to go into her usual temper tantrum when in despair I said, 'You know, I feel like having a tantrum sometimes, too.' This stopped her and she asked, unbelievingly, 'You do?'

"I told her I felt so inadequate to teach some of the things she needed to know, because I'm not very good at them myself. And then she made me really wonder when she asked, 'When I grow up, will I be like you?'

"I answered, 'Oh, honey, you probably will.' But Fran answered, 'I'm glad,' as she ran out the door. Since that day we have had a new rapport. She began helping me help her and neither of us has thrown a fit since."

Such books and courses as Parent Effectiveness Training (*P.E.T.*) by Dr. Thomas Gordon are helpful in learning how to problem-solve through active listening rather than through adult-imposed decisions.

This idea is expressed eloquently by an eleven-year-old girl in a note left under her father's pillow.

Children have feelings just like adults. When a child's feelings are hurt they usually keep it to themselves.

In school if you have a seemingly mean teacher you can't

always share your ideas with her as a friend. So you do what she says and do it how she says.

Some problems adults don't seem to understand and get the wrong idea. I have very understanding parents and I can discuss my problems with them without their telling me what I have to do.

Children will react favorably in an environment that is happy and relaxed, where they are accepted as they are, their opinions valued. They will be more willing to work on deficiencies and be tolerant of those who do not understand if they "catch" a positive attitude, one of hope and encouragement, from their first and best teachers—the parents.

CHAPTER V

A House of Learning

A responsibility of parents is to develop a love of learning and to serve as the link between education and the real world. The imagination of children needs to be released, deficiencies improved, and pent-up energy channeled in constructive ways.

Parents sometimes take the position that it is the school's responsibility to teach the skills, or they go to the other extreme and make the home too school-like. Reinforcement of formal teaching or even the total training may take place at home, but the activities can be made fun and rewarding and different. This is especially important for a child who is not understanding or cannot perform as expected.

Activities must be chosen that are relevant to the needs of the child. Unless a youngster's maturity is sufficient in all areas—physical, mental, emotional, and social—he will feel pressure if he is forced into reading, math, or other learning experiences for which he is unready. So games and equipment should be chosen to emphasize listening, to improve motor functioning, to develop reasoning and memory, or whatever is needed.

Every child should be read to from books, but the usual materials do not have to be used to teach reading.

A recent newspaper article was titled "Comic Books Are

Good for Them." The article told about a comic book aimed specifically at teaching children to read better. It is called "Spidey" and is produced in cooperation with The Electric Company and Marvel Comics. It can be bought at the newsstand as can others about famous people and events.

Reading can also be taught from the newspaper, cereal boxes, cake mixes, and so forth. Words can be written on cards and placed as labels on objects. However, sight recognition may not be the problem. Hearing the sounds or remembering how to spell the words or understanding the meanings may be the greater concern.

Mathematics does not belong in the classroom alone. There is calculation in cooking, in building, in laying an obstacle course, in buying something good to eat, in planning a trip. Parents can do much to reduce the fear of math, or what has been called mathophobia. A retractable tape measure makes an excellent gift.

Hyperactivity needs careful management. Most of these children have short attention spans, and the family plans must take this into account. Other family members have to be considered also so that the aggressive member does not dominate everything they do. There needs to be more than the usual amount of play materials and a variety of activities provided in order to channel the excessive energy.

Above all the child must be successful. This does not mean avoiding activities that he cannot do. Parents can watch for situations that are not handled well and help as needed. The end results need to be pleasurable. Learning math or new words through cooking becomes enjoyable when what is made can be eaten.

Kinesthetic and Tactile Learning

Kinesthesia is "the perception of sensations received through the muscles and joints and nerve endings." *Kinesthetic* refers to "movement." So kinesthetic learning that involves tactility, the sense of touch, is that which comes through all of the body, through movement and exploration, touching and feeling.

Many people learn best this way, and some require the reinforcement of touch or movement to remember. Since most formal teaching emphasizes the visual and auditory channels, this type of teaching must not be neglected by the parent.

Motor involvement is therapeutic. Often the body will remember what the mind forgets.

Suggestions include:

—walking outlines of letters and words.

—acting out meanings of words—such as *running* and *hopping*—of concrete nouns as well as abstract ideas

—manipulating objects for counting and other computations.

—writing on the child's back or arm or guiding him into forming words in the air. Helen Keller was taught by writing in her hand.

—moving and feeling letters and forming them into words. Letters can be shaped from clay or cooked dough, of yarn, pipestem cleaners, glue, or sandpaper.

Writing can be done with the finger in fingerpaint, sand, on a blackboard or feltboard, or in chocolate syrup.

Probably no disability is more persistent and annoying than

inconsistent spelling. The kinesthetic approach is helpful in reducing spelling errors and in reversal problems.

The child should not learn the word just by copying it and should never be allowed to write it incorrectly. He might first study the word, saying it aloud. Then make the word out of a raised material and trace over it with a finger as he repeats it. Or he could trace one written by an adult in the sand or on a blackboard. Closing his eyes, he then traces the word with his finger on the material or writes it in the air. Finally it is written from memory with a pencil or pen.

The Kitchen: A Center of Learning

The kitchen is the place to measure, stir, decide amounts, compare sizes, use different instruments, play with canned goods, et cetera. The child who is clumsy in the kitchen and thus not allowed to help may be the one who would benefit the most. Parents have to exert the patience they expect others to have when working with their children.

Some of the learning things a child may do are:

—Make rolled cookie dough. Rolling out the dough is good for hand coordination. Cut triangles, squares, circles. Talk about the shapes while working—and eating. Cut the dough into narrow strips and shape into letters or words. Bake them.

—Make fingerpaint. Materials: 1/3 cup laundry starch
2 cups boiling water
½ cup gentle soap flakes
food coloring or poster paint
small jars

Dissolve the starch in a little cold water. Then stir in the boiling water. Cook over low heat, stirring constantly, until clear and thick. Remove from heat. Stir in soap flakes. Pour into several jars. Add a different color to each jar. Paint on white freezer paper. Write in the paint with a finger. Practice drawing shapes. Prepare for cursive writing by making continuous lines and strokes without picking up the finger. Progress to dipping a sponge into the paint and writing on newspaper.

—Make clay dough.   Mix together: ½ cup salt
1 cup plain flour
1 tsp. powdered alum
(may be omitted)
Add: 1 Tbs. vegetable oil
Stir in: 1 cup boiling water
Stir vigorously until mixture holds together.

Knead the dough until smooth.

Divide into several lumps. Add a few drops of food coloring or poster paint to make desired color, and knead to mix.

Store in airtight container. Will dry in open air in a few days or can be baked at 200° F for about an hour.

Shape letters out of the clay dough. Put together to make words. Press clay into flat pan, and write in it with a sharp stick.

—With a dull pencil write words in styrofoam meat trays or tops of egg cartons.

—Guess how many marshmallows, dried beans, or pieces of bread in a package. Count them.

—Guess which container holds the most. Measure many different shapes and sizes against one another. Use a marked container to tell exactly how much is in each. Choose appropriately sized containers to store food.

—Choose four round containers and draw around them— two square ones, one rectangle, and others. Notice other shapes in the kitchen.

—Grease cake and other pans, touching all the corners, not stopping all the way around.

—Stir something twenty times, or another suitable number, before licking the spoon.

—Estimate how long an activity will take and set the timer to check.

—Set up a store with canned goods, alternately buying and selling.

—Arrange unbreakable utensils into the lower cabinets by shapes, sizes, various uses.

—Practice pouring by using dry materials first—rice, macaroni—then pour liquids.

—Make one complete part of the meal. Start with a prepared mix like muffins and then something like creamed potatoes. Estimate how many potatoes are needed and peel them.

—Cut words off mix and cereal boxes and arrange them into sentences.

—An adult can assist further by giving oral instructions so the child must listen in order to proceed. Have the child pretend to be a television cook. Write down what he says and then help him learn the words and read his own directions.

For the hyperactive child and others who need snacks, have on hand high-protein foods. The child can be encouraged to count twenty-five peanuts, cut cheese into small pieces, and make and spread peanut butter.

—Raw peanuts, baked lightly in a low oven and shelled, can be ground in a blender with a little bit of oil.

The Dining Room

—A family member can give oral directions for setting the table, first, one at a time, then increase to two or more: "put the glass on the right of the plate, at the top of the knife." Also give a direction that is incorrect to see if the child notices what is wrong. For example: six knives, four spoons, eight forks.

—A table set with a plain cloth and sturdy glasses reduces spilling and helps a highly distractible child to concentrate.

—The child can fold napkins into different shapes and place them as instructed.

—Math can be practiced by having the child cut the pie into halves, then fourths. The youngster can decide how many rolls each will have if there are a dozen in the basket.

—Practicing good conversational habits while the family is together at the table, results in a stronger unity but also does much to improve expression of ideas.

The Living Room

—Act out social situations, play charades.
—Read and discuss stories, Draw pictures to illustrate.

—Play quiet games of all kinds. If the child cannot play a game that others in the family or his friends enjoy, it can be taught in steps, perhaps apart from the main games. Consider the concepts that are not understood. For example, to play checkers requires understanding of *diagonal, up, down, across, in front of,* and *behind,* color, and so forth. It also demands some manual dexterity, forces the child to think and plan. Many children lack these skills.

—Follow-the-dot pictures can be used to teach numbers in sequence.

—Puzzles from the simplest to the most complicated help children notice shape and look for missing parts of a picture.

—Listening to the radio and record or tape player strengthens auditory skills. Too much television viewing encourages the child to rely overly on visual stimulation.

—Talking through puppets is helpful in expressing anger, happiness, discontent if these are difficult to express otherwise. It also encourages creativity through imagination.

Interesting magazines provide exciting learning, particularly ones about the natural sciences.

The Bedroom

A child's bedroom can facilitate learning and add to a sense of security. It should be an orderly place, as uncluttered as possible and easy to straighten. Plain curtains and bedspread, toys out of sight and only a few teaching aids visible at the time keep hyperactivity to a minimum and encourages good organization. The occupant should choose the colors that are pleasing.

Some children feel more secure with the bed against the wall. Many need to have an adult lie down with them and read or sing until their motors run down and their little bodies can sleep.

Children should never be locked into a closed room, but some early risers need to be contained until others are astir in the house. A Dutch door (one that has an upper and lower half that opens separately) which has a center shelf protruding into the room is helpful. The top half can be left open and the lower part locked. The shelf helps keep the child from climbing out.

The child, with help from someone in the family, can make a chart of what is to be done and when. For the young child this could include an order for dressing: Pictures of the correct order can be posted.

If a child is learning to tell time, the chart could be a large clock drawn on paper. Leave off the minute hand until the hour hand is understood. If the clock can be put on the floor, the child could jump from hour to hour and discuss what happens each time. Or with the clock on the wall, he can swing an arm around.

—An hourglass helps convey the passing of time. As does a monthly calendar on which to mark off the days.

—An outdoor thermometer on the window and an indoor one encourage the keeping of daily records.

—A large mirror is useful for learning body parts and for studying mirror images. The child needs to understand that left and right remain the same within no matter which way the person is facing.

—Signs posted on the four walls of the room help establish north, south, east, and west.

—Large maps or illustrated geography lessons help make concrete the sense of distance.

—The bedroom is an ideal place to keep a supply of glue, yarn, and pipestem cleaners so that spelling words can be practiced in a different way each night. A blackboard is essential.

—A tape or record player can provide soothing music as well as provide other learning experiences.

—Fleece balls and hoops and bean bags to throw into trash baskets or paper bags help improve visual and motor coordination. Bean bags are easily made by children.

—Games of many kinds, particularly building sets, should be available.

—Hobbies and collections add a great deal to learning. Coin and stamp collections are especially good. A simple camera and a photograph album encourage many new learning experiences.

The Bathroom

Have the child estimate the length of time he showers. Set a timer to check. If he bathes in the tub, how much water does he use? Can it be measured in volume or depth?

Is the child longer than the bath mat? How much does he weigh? Keep a record of weight, height, distance around the waist.

What are the dimensions of the bathroom? The tub?

The mirror can be used to practice saying words and to see how they are formed. Call attention to the fact that similar sounds require the same formation.

Instructions posted on the mirror are not easily overlooked. Signs can be posted where the towels hang, on the toothbrush holder, and so on.

The Garage

The garage is a place to build and discover relationships, to practice using tools and putting things in their correct places, and to make equipment to be used elsewhere.

This can be done by:

—building a bird house. Draw a pattern on a piece of paper, list the materials needed. Follow the plan.

—making a nail board. Choose a board at least one foot square or larger. Arrange ten rows of ten nails about an inch or more apart. Different colored rubber bands can be stretched from nail to nail to make squares and other shapes, to count by twos, tens, and so on, and to teach multiplication.

—mixing chemical solutions. Soda and vinegar make an interesting combination.

—making puppets, even the stage. They can be made out of sticks with faces pasted on, of paper bags with faces colored in, or of the more complicated papier-mâché.

—binding a screen wire for writing a raised imprint. Cut a fine wire about eight by eleven inches. Tape the edges with masking or furniture tape. Place a piece of paper on top of the screen and with a crayon write the words to be learned. Remove the screen, and trace over the words with a finger.

—sorting or counting nails, screws and other supplies, dirty laundry, and game equipment.

The Backyard

The yard can provide exciting and unlimited possibilities for learning. It is a place to:
—grow a garden;
—feed the birds and listen to the sounds of nature;
—practice spelling by writing in the sand;
—plan and lay out an obstacle course. Build a set of steps to go over, plan tunnels to go through, boards to walk on, something to climb, large tires to jump on.
—paint large areas. Use fingerpaint. It will wash off.
—allow a junk corner. Provide old radios and appliances to take apart, wires to string up, and whatever else the imagination can put together from salvaged materials.
—build a fort or tree house.
—dig holes and fill them in when finished playing.
—play games. Tetherball and croquet help eye-hand coordination. Starting with bean bags or large balls, throw these into a circle on the ground, or hit them with a flat board. Catch bean bags, large balls, then small ones. After proficiency in all of these is exhibited, play with the regular bat and ball.
—measure everything—the trees, the distances around and across the yard, how far is a jump or a thrown ball.

A house can be large or small, it doesn't matter. If a few materials are provided and a lot of guidance, the disabled child will make his own adjustments to his problems and will emerge a whole person. A sense of humor is also helpful.

Tommy's parents were trying to teach him the value of money. To cut down on his spending, they had him keep an exact account of how he spent his allowance each week. One day, he remarked to them, "You know, since I have to write everything down, I really stop and think before I buy things."

The parents were congratulating themselves silently when Tommy continued, "I just don't buy anything that's hard to spell."

CHAPTER VI

Home and School Working Together

"A pupil's image of himself is reflected in his progress in school," states a report card. It might also add that often a parent's image of himself is reflected by his child's progress in school.

Everyone involved is affected by poor marks. Frequently the tendency is to blame one another. The parent says of the teacher, "Why isn't he teaching my child?" The teacher sighs, "If the parents would only cooperate—" The child tells his friends, "The teacher's really against me. I'm out of it here and at home, especially when they see my report card."

Another reaction is to blame oneself, with the parents wondering if they should have been more strict and teachers feeling that they failed somewhere. The child says of himself, "Boy, I must be dumb."

Now with the knowledge that no one really is at fault for the learning differences of these children, the defensive attitude is waning, and cooperation has become the key to success.

The initiative, however, may lie with the parent.

The Parent Approaches the School

The attitude with which the parent comes to the school helps set the stage for how much progress is possible.

69

Teachers cannot be expected to know all that they may need to know about teaching children with learning problems. Only in recent years have there been courses available to train teachers about the recognition and remediation of learning disabilities, and many colleges still do not offer them. Anyone desiring this training often must obtain it on his own time, if it is available, often while carrying a full load of regular responsibilities as well.

Large classes in our children's schools make it difficult to give the attention needed to special concerns. Every teacher would like to have more time with the individuals in the class.

Teaching a child with these subtle learning problems *is* difficult. There is no magic key to punch that will release the potential imprisoned within these youngsters. Mistakes are made, and the patience of all involved is exhausted at times. But teachers are trying as well as are the parents.

Parents must not infer that teachers do not know how to teach. A teacher knows many things that parents need to hear.

Working with the child, adults at school and at home determine the amount of homework that can be done, the proper grade placement, and the solutions to a myriad number of other problems that arise.

A parent can establish a tone of confidence and enthusiasm which may be contagious.

However, there are occasions when a teacher will not listen and when parents must decide that an uninformed or uncooperative person cannot determine the future of their children.

Then comes the greatest test because in some cases little

can be done except better to provide for the child's needs at home and help make the best of the situation.

Adjusting to an unsatisfactory setting is sometimes to be preferred to shifting the child unless there is certainty of success elsewhere. This adjustment, though not easy, can be a valuable learning experience.

So then bad grades may have to be overlooked and activities provided outside of school to bolster the child's ego and develop his talents. The warmth of family love and understanding helps a child develop inner strength and enables him to work out his own problems.

If the pressures are too great and the adjustments do not provide enough relief, placement in another class should be considered. Parents may have to exert pressure to get this done, perhaps even securing a statement from a doctor. The child should not be made to suffer through and perhaps lose a whole school year.

So then a parent must:

1. be informed.

A parent must seek understanding of all aspects of learning disabilities before he can hope to explain it to another. Knowledge of the terminology, of informative reading materials, and of available films is helpful.

2. not approach defensively or guiltily.

Parents have a right to know what is going on in school, and all children have the right to an education no matter how severe a disability. While parents should not blame themselves for the child's condition, they do have to shoulder part of the responsibility for their children's getting an adequate education.

Certainly empathy is in order for a teacher who must guide

and teach a hyperkinetic child all day. He is a handful for the parent and will be for a teacher, as are those with many other traits shown by students who must struggle so to succeed.

If a child does not listen to a parent at home, he may not be able to listen to the teacher. If he is unruly, too quiet, exasperating, he will show these traits in school.

If a parent can agree with the teacher that they share a difficult situation, the way is cleared for frankness and teamwork.

3. tell the teacher what the child can and likes to do as well as what he cannot do.

Sensitive feelings can be approached cautiously so that the teacher does not step where it hurts and the relationship can begin on a positive note.

4. listen to what the teacher says.

He observes things that a parent misses or cannot see because children show some different behaviors in school. The teacher can see progress when a parent feels there is none. Parents are apt to get overwrought and to imagine problems that do not exist or are common to normal youngsters at that age. Advice to "let him go. He'll find himself" may need to be heeded at times.

5. take the pressure off.

Children with learning problems should not be evaluated as is the average child, but they usually are. Grades of D and F become rather common.

The parents' attitude toward these school-issued reports will help determine whether they undermine the efforts of the child. Many children who are learning well cannot give back information required on tests. Others work hard and make excellent progress but may still be below grade level.

Report-card day need not be traumatic if the parents do not get upset. Ask for a more realistic accounting of the student's achievements at regular intervals so that progress, which may not be evident in the grades, can be acknowledged.

If a child is not achieving or seems not to be trying, additional pressures usually cause emotional stress and do little to improve the deficient learning. Different approaches are needed and time away from the unpleasant tasks. Most of all, a level at which he can succeed must be established.

These children need time, sometimes years, even with the best of help, in which to overcome some disabilities.

6. provide for needs not met in school.

Children need time alone, time to do nothing. Parents should expect tension to build up and provide opportunity for the tension to be released. Tutoring may be needed. Training in art, music, sports, or whatever interests the child helps develop a strong self-concept.

Establish a routine homework time. Many things, to be retained, must be repeated and practiced in different ways. There is not enough time in school for this. Parents can keep up with what is being studied and can help reinforce the learning at home. Or they can teach that which was missed through the kinesthetic approach and other experiences that may be too time-consuming to be done in the classroom. If learning at school is boring, it can be made more interesting at home.

Jan was failing miserably on spelling tests and in other written work where spelling was being marked off. Her mother read about the use of tactile materials and decided to try teaching Jan that way at home. After several weeks, her mother wrote a friend:

73

I've been meaning to write for several weeks to let you know of Jan's progress. But just when I was going to do so with a glowing report, she brought home three *D*s in a row. However, I discovered it was not the words she learned to spell with her finger. She had spelled nearly all the words I had taught her correctly and missed ⅔ of the ones from a list of "good speller" words which the teacher throws in. So we started in on those.

Now she frequently catches herself in the midst of making a wrong letter and says, "No, that's wrong." Once she knew she had spelled the word incorrectly but didn't know what mistake she had made.

I must say it gets discouraging at times, and we both tire of it. Still, I see the progress, so we'll keep at it.

7. not baby a child with learning disabilities.

He will have to learn that some things are acceptable to some people and some places but not always. He must learn to obey even when he does not always understand or agree.

A student with learning problems must learn to work hard, harder than others. Many have become great achievers because things were never easy, and they learned to struggle and compensate at an early age.

While sympathy and understanding are important, the child must not be excused because she has a problem and be allowed to give up. Neither should all pathways be laid out by adults. The child who is most successful finds his own way of dealing with the difficulties.

Rudy in first grade turned in a paper that looked like this:

$$ 7 \; 7 \; 7 \; \lceil \; \lceil \; \lceil $$

Of course, the teacher marked three of them as being incorrect. When his mother asked what those three were he answered, "Well, I knew a seven went one way or another, but I couldn't remember which. So I put three one way and three the other. That way," he explained patiently, " I knew I would get half of them right."

8. observe, listen, converse.

A child's actions may reveal that things are worse than what is said, but what he tells may need only to be listened to. Feelings should not be kept locked within, though some of it may not be pleasant to hear. Parents should not be overly upset by some of the language used or expressions of discontent. This may be the child's way of dealing with his frustrations, and he would not want interference by the parents.

Encourage talking about events and relationships. Sometimes that is all that is needed for the child to be able to face another day of hard work. Parents should refrain from too much advice or so many admonitions that a child avoids the conversation. Even too much questioning can be detrimental.

In the Classroom

Even if there were enough good special teachers for these children, their problems would not be over. They are and should be in the regular classroom most of the time.

There are many adjustments that can be made within the schoolday to help a child learn better, to find out what he has learned, and to inspire him to keep trying.

Dwelling too much upon what may have caused the present may impede progress and may even be erroneous.

HELPING CHILDREN WITH LEARNING DISABILITIES

Family instability may be at the root of many learning and emotional problems, but it is also true that a child who has never succeeded in school can be a contributing or causative factor in the instability. Lessening of the stress in the educational setting can be good for the whole family.

It is not safe to assume that a student who does not listen well watches too much television; that one who cannot sit still is undisciplined; or that peculiar character traits are the result of too little attention at home.

Connie, in talking to the classroom teacher about her son's low reading level, was told, "Parents don't read to their children anymore. That's why we have so many slow readers now."

"Oh, but I do," Connie protested. "I always have—nearly every night," she emphasized.

So she was referred to the guidance counselor who was told that the mother read a great deal to the child. The counselor explained away the shortcoming with the assumption, "You are reading too much. Make Larry read to himself."

Nor is it wise to infer that a student isn't trying or could do the work if he would. Perhaps he can't. Fear of failure and poor habits based upon inadequate skills restrict appropriate responses.

In the accompanying example are the answers wrong or just backward? How confused a child would be in his understanding of math if daily his answers were marked as being incorrect when he was sure that four plus two equals six, and three and two are five.

Usually a child does not understand why his answers are

Find the sums.

3 + 3 = 9 ✗	1 + 5 = 0 ✗
4 + 1 = 2 ⁵	6 + 0 = 4 ✗
4 + 2 = 0 ⁶	0 + 6 = 0 ✗
1 + 1 = 2	2 + 3 = 2 ✗
2 + 4 = 0 ✗	2 + 4 = 0 ✗
3 + 3 = 0 ✗	4 + 2 = 0 ✗
5 + 1 = 0 ✗	5 + 0 = 2 ✗
1 + 2 = 3	3 + 3 = 0 ✗
2 + 2 = 4	4 + 1 = 2 ✗
2 + 4 = 0 ✗	4 + 2 = 0 ✗

marked wrong when they are reversed or cannot stop himself from making the errors. He does, however, understand and feel the effect of red marks, reprimands, and ill will.

No child can withstand the experience of constant failure without becoming terribly discouraged, feeling inadequate or angry and aggressive. All children develop some cover to draw attention away from their inadequacies—a ''don't care'' attitude, becoming a show-off, or simply doing something other than the impossible task.

A teacher's theme for setting up a healing and instructive

atmosphere should be to utilize a child's strengths while, if possible, improving the deficiencies.

1. Don't judge ability of learning-disabled children by achievement-test scores. Many learning-disabled students never do well on tests of any kind, especially standardized ones. Extremely low scores of a seemingly average child are indications of needs rather than ability. The need may involve a different kind of testing, for the pupil may have the information but cannot give it back quickly enough or cannot put the answers in the proper places.

2. Analyze the student's work and behaviors with assumptions laid aside. Even if a thorough professional evaluation is available, it will not be enough. An observant teacher/parent/child combination can put together a helpful dossier.

Keep a record of what the student does or cannot do. Note patterns of response: poor organization, inadequate planning, tiring, or giving up easily. Discover which style of learning seems strongest, the auditory, visual, or kinesthetic.

An analysis of fifty words misspelled by a child will reveal the types of errors made most consistently—sequencing or reversals errors, letters omitted perhaps because the child does not hear that particular sound, poor recall because he cannot revisualize words.

Most of all, discover what the child can do well. Remediation must come through his interests.

Many teachers find that this kind of observation and analysis of a child's classroom performance is no more time-consuming than the constant reprimands and correcting of mistakes and is a lot more productive.

3. Teach the pupil in spite of his handicap. Even though a

student cannot read he may be able to learn the material if it is read to him, by another child, perhaps. He may learn the math principles and understand computation even if he cannot read or if he is allowed concrete materials.

Many learning-disabled children are able to memorize or recall some things but may have poor memories for symbols or numerical facts. They may be unable to memorize the multiplication tables. These children need a copy of the tables in order to complete math assignments. Memorization exercises should not prevent progress.

If spelling errors or poor handwriting are characteristic, count off for the mistakes only in spelling or writing exercises. Do not spoil an interest in science or creative writing by concentrating upon the mistakes related to something else.

Allow a pupil to learn in ways most suitable to him. Some children cannot pick up on oral instructions or assignments well enough or remember them long enough to accomplish a task. They need to be written. A child can be helped to realize that he has a weakness here and that he must write notes to himself, but he must first understand what the assignment is.

Often a teacher explains that a pupil wasn't paying attention or he would have heard the homework assignment, while the student declares that he didn't hear her give any homework.

While remediation must be done in the auditory channel, if that is the weakest area, or in the visual, learning can go on if allowances are made for these deficits, and multisensory teaching takes place.

There is no need to keep moving ahead if the work or skill

is not mastered. However, there is no reason to hold a child back in everything until he masters a technique or acquires an understanding that may take months or years to conquer. Allow him to go forward in areas in which he is competent.

This is why retaining a student with learning disabilities in a grade often is not successful. Their development is uneven, and they may be so far ahead in some things as to be bored. Unless expert help is available they will not progress in the weak areas.

The degree of maturity and the allowances for individual needs determine grade placement. Rarely do these children fit into the average groupings, and mere repetition of a year's work does little to meet their needs.

A person with learning difficulties must be made to work, really work on specific problems, but that must not affect everything that has to be done.

4. Teach through a positive approach. When only the bad behavior is noticed and only the mistakes marked, negative attitudes are reinforced.

Laura brought home paper after paper with many marked mistakes that she would not discuss with her mother. Finally her mother said. "Laura, how can I help you if you won't let me show you what you have done wrong?"

Miserably Laura answered, "But I can't stand to look at my papers with all those red marks."

Where there are obviously a lot of mistakes on a paper, attention should be directed to the correct answers. Valuable encouragement can be given by marking how many were correct yesterday, how many today and by setting a goal with the child for tomorrow. Score points for progress.

Kyle consistently missed sixteen or more out of twenty words on the weekly spelling test and made a *D* each time. He agreed to learn them tactically at home. Night after night he worked and missed only thirteen, finally, but still made a *D*. Then he missed eight but still a *D*.

One day he came home with only six or seven missed, and as he walked in the door, he threw his paper at his mother and said, "I'm not working anymore at home. It doesn't matter how many I miss. She never notices, just keeps on giving me *D*s."

Kyle's father wrote a note to the teacher calling attention to the fact that Kyle had improved from missing most of the words to missing six or seven. Shouldn't he have a better grade?

The teacher wrote a cryptic note in return, "If Kyle missed six, he should have made a *C*, but I counted seven missed and this is a *D*."

Kyle never studied spelling at home again.

Children who are sitting quietly in their seats need to be noticed if that is the behavior expected, particularly if doing so is difficult.

A child who has many problems that are constantly being noticed needs to have his good qualities, his efforts and progress emphasized if he is to feel any degree of self-worth. If effort and correct answers are noticed, the child will try harder to achieve this recognition.

5. Test a child the way he can give the most information. For some children this means an oral test, given by another student, if necessary. For others it means allowing extra time or presenting the material on posters or in booklets. Some children cannot organize and write booklets, make posters, or take oral tests.

Many students respond well on multiple-choice exams because they recognize the words needed but cannot recall them unaided. Undecipherable printing or duplicated papers are often stumbling blocks to a poor reader.

The result of the same exam given the rest of the class should not determine a grade for a student who has learning disabilities.

6. Communicate with parents. Adults in the home can reinforce and add to the classroom activities if they know what is needed. Children who are not doing well in school rarely communicate this. There are many additional suggestions in the teacher's manuals that parents can do at home.

A student who has a learning disability should not be graded on a scale comparing him to other children in the class. He should be graded in terms of his own progress, and his performance should be evaluated in light of his specific disabilities. Frequent and specific reports are needed, including statements of improvements. Parents as well as students need to know that there is progress.

7. The set-up of the classroom may contribute to learning or may add to the child's difficulties, especially for distractible and unorganized children. Too much clutter, confusion, or noise add to the predicament of a child who has trouble concentrating or working diligently.

A private "office" space where a child can withdraw by choice to be alone or to work uninterrupted may be necessary.

A posted schedule is important for many children, with changes carefully explained in advance. Activities within the day need to be carefully structured with shorter periods of participation for some children and longer periods of varied learning for others. Children with learning handicaps rarely are able to make choices of what to do when and need a great deal of help in using their time wisely, in knowing where to start and how to proceed.

Many different types of materials—manipulative, tactile, audio, and visual—contribute to learning through all of the senses.

8. The hyperkinetic student needs special adjustments in the day's routine. He may need a snack in midmorning. A change of activity is helpful, but this does not mean running around the school or running an extra lap around the playground. These restless youngsters seem to have a lot of energy, but much of it is nervous tension which causes tiredness. Extreme physical effort may only increase irritability. Some can be allowed to draw while listening to a story or to do macrame.

Difficult tasks can be broken into short assignments with goals established to work longer or more carefully or quietly. Positive and encouraging comments help keep them at the task.

9. Encourage developmental programs for playground time, not just calisthenics, games, or free play. Ego strength can be improved or damaged during physical education time.

Inefficient movement hampers a child whether or not learning problems accompany it. Motor activities can add to efforts initiated in the classroom because memory, body awareness, abstract concepts, problem-solving, and many other primary learning opportunities are involved.

10. Do pass on helpful information to the next teacher. These students face each new term with more than the usual apprehension. Much of this could be alleviated if the new teacher is aware of the dysfunctions, the learning styles, the

talents. Otherwise, valuable time is lost while these are being rediscovered.

11. Love and understanding must be expressed toward the child no matter how much he may try one's patience.

Tim was given some very good tutoring and became a much better student. He expressed his feelings this way: "My teacher used to not like me. Now that I'm doing better she does. But I'm the same me," he explained.

Children with the variety of problems called learning disabilities usually struggle along in school. Few enjoy it. The days can be made more enjoyable as well as fruitful if their uniqueness is recognized and they are not judged by the performances of others.

How children see and approach tasks differently can be seen in this illustration.

Wishing to test her children's powers of deduction, a teacher told them to write down what they would think if they went into a room and found cobwebs there. Each child in the class, except one, gave her the answer she had hoped for; that the room had not been dusted lately; that it had not been in use; that the person responsible was dirty and lazy. Wendy's answer was sublime in its simplicity and refusal to jump to fanciful conclusions. She wrote, "A spider had been there."

CHAPTER VII

The Adolescent

Does the teen-ager who cannot read or the one who does not do well in school become a responsible adult? Should college be considered? Is the high-school or young-adult age too late to make up the lost learning?

For many, already it may be too late. Recent studies show that 70 to 80 percent of juvenile delinquents of average and above average intelligence have learning handicaps. Many mental breakdowns have the roots in school failures and, of course, a large number of the bright youths who drop out of school do so because of the losing struggle to succeed.

Mark, a learning-disabled student already a year behind, was thrown out of parochial school when he was in the seventh grade because he would not cut his hair and acted surly toward his teacher. He never quite made it into public school.

His mother, a widow with a younger, severely handicapped nonreader, was called by the school frequently because of Mark's absenteeism and fighting on the school grounds. The police first called because of a minor disturbance, then a break-in. The calls from the school and the police became more frequent.

Mark dropped school completely when he was fifteen. His mother confided to her minister, "He sleeps through the day and roams around at night. I don't know what to do with him," she said.

What next is in store for Mark?

Sharon, a bright, attractive student popular in school activities, worked hard for her grades. She learned fast and could read well. As she advanced in school, it became apparent that she was giving mostly rote responses and did not understand much of the work. The pressure to keep up her grades so that she could remain a cheerleader became too much.

Sharon had a mental breakdown in the ninth grade and spent the next two years in and out of hospitals, in a rehabilitation center, or lying around the house. She tried school a couple of times after that but could not face her former friends, and there was still no remedial help available. She has moved from job to job since.

Alice could read at about the second-grade level. She quit high school at sixteen and a year later married. There were problems with shopping, checks, and recipes; so Alice went to night school. She was still required to read, and since she couldn't, this final attempt was abandoned also.

After her baby was born, Alice called her mother in tears one day because she could not read the directions on a bottle of medicine. "Will he grow up like me and not be able to read either?" Alice asked, sobbing.

Avery, who could not read, ran away from home with a friend who had no school problems but did have a very unhappy home life.

While Avery and his parents were driving the four hundred miles back home, there was time for long conversation. "Why did you go—are things that bad at our house?" questioned the parents.

"No," Avery explained earnestly, "it's not at home. But I

86

had to go with him, don't you see?'' he pleaded. "Mack does all my reading for me. Nobody else knows I can't read.''

Few can imagine the heartache and confusion faced by a young adult who cannot read or keep an account of his finances. Undecipherable are notes from girl or boy friends, menus in restaurants, telephone books, signs—even necessary ones when labeled cutely like Mickey and Minnie or Squaw and Brave—directions on machines and packages, driver's-license tests as well as the television listings and movie information.

The common disturbances of the adolescent stage—the turmoil and erratic behavior, the emotional ups and downs, the reckless and impulsive actions—are magnified in a youth with learning disabilities.

"Adolescents with severe learning problems may divert so much energy into hiding or trying to cope with their disabilities that they have little time or energy left for the tasks of adolescence—to establish a positive self-image, to come to terms with sexuality, to set long-range vocational goals, and to meet society's demands,'' states the film *Adolescence and Learning Disability* (see Resources).

After years of struggling to succeed in school, many simply give up. The demands are too great, and there is even less understanding now because few secondary schools are prepared to deal with these hidden handicaps.

A teen-ager expressed well the feelings of many when he said, "I just get tired, emotionally tired, from making *D*s and *F*s day after day when I have worked so hard.''

Amazingly, however, many are still fighting to succeed. Some have made it. For them it was not and is not too late.

Rob, introduced in chapter 3, received no appropriate help

until he was in the seventh grade. He struggled through the junior high years with the help of a tutor. His mother read homework aloud.

High school was very difficult also, but he knew his problem and was willing to work hard. Rob was happy in outside pursuits of scouting, riflery, and water sports.

Forced to attend a community college because of his low grades, Rob, however, found an excitement in learning that he had not known before and insisted on taking extra courses each semester. He maintained high grades even while taking chemistry, logic, English, physics, and many computer courses. His only real difficulty was with algebra, which he took four times before passing.

Rob graduated with honors and is attending a senior-division college of his choice to major in computer science. He talks of working toward getting a master's degree.

His mother writes, "Rob has 'eaten up' all the computer work he's had. They call him 'Teach' and have him fix the computers frequently when mechanical trouble pops up. He has even worked out programs for others and has devised games to play on it."

Quiet Patty, in chapter 2, is still that way and has few friends. Math eludes her, but she makes good grades in everything else. She seems to be a happy girl and plays the violin in the community orchestra.

While hyperactive Rusty, always bored with school, has played on the winning baseball teams. He is attending vocational school, learning to be a mechanic and loves his after-school job at a service station. Rusty is a mature, self-reliant young adult.

Stan hated reading until high school when, as his father

said, "He seemed to just start one day and enjoyed it." He graduated very low in his class but went on to college. Even though he has worked very hard, he never received a degree because he cannot pass English courses.

While still in college he was hired by a large electric company and soon advanced to a supervisory position because of his genius in seeing through the workings of new models. "I'll get that degree yet!" Stan declares.

Nora married young after dropping out of school because she had failed so many times. When her son was in the third grade and was diagnosed as being learning disabled, her efforts at finding help for him led her to the realization that his problems were similar to the ones she had experienced in school.

Determination renewed, she applied to take the high-school equivalency exam after having her husband read the books to her. She requested the cooperative examiners to give the test orally. "I could always learn anything I could hear, and I can tell it to you better," she explained.

Then in her enthusiasm she enrolled in a junior college which specializes in multi-media teaching. She is planning to be a teacher for children affected as she was.

Nora declares, "I don't want anyone going through what I did." Now she says excitedly, "Oh, it's like being reborn."

The difference between eventual success and dropping out, juvenile delinquency, or breakdown seems to lie in the quality of help received, how much pressure is applied by school and home, and whether some special skill is developed.

Many youths tend to outgrow their difficulties and make

their own adjustments if demands have not been too great and if there is support from persons around them.

However, they may not acquire the missing skill—reading particularly—without specialized instruction, and there has been little of this in most secondary-school systems. Most regular remedial reading classes have done little to help because of the lack of knowledge of specific learning disabilities.

The difficulties of children with these problems often tend to bring out strengths beyond the average child. This is seen in the many creative endeavors of children and youths who are not good students as such.

Primarily, though, success in school is a required component for continuing growth. Several points need to be considered in planning an individual educational program.

1. The basic deficiency may still exist and will need remediation before progress in that area can be expected.

If sequencing—putting letters or numbers in a continuing order—is still not understood, it may have to be taught by making bracelets, working with peg boards, or playing games. However, the application must be made to reading or math as well. This and other concepts are elemental, and most children do not have to be instructed in these things. They notice and learn on their own. On the other hand, some never do learn and must be taught at whatever age the deficiency manifests itself.

The same is true of any of the primary concepts—the differentiation of the main figure from the background; the constancy of a number or letter being the same no matter how it's turned or what size or style of print; the internal sense of direction, size, and amounts, so important to mathematical functioning—are all so basic as to be ignored in planning instruction for the older student but are crippling in their absence.

For many students the sounds of the classroom are to them like listening in on a foreign-language class. They catch some of it but miss more. The fundamental skill of word analysis, blending, even the application of simple rules are elusive. Many still do not realize the relationship of the sound of a word to its printed form.

Much of the work habits did not develop gradually as with other children. At the secondary level, the student is expected to be on his own to get work done, but the need for structure and guidance still exists for the adolescent with a learning disability.

The lack of organizing and planning ability hampers homework and other assignments. A quarterly report of a learning-disabled youth usually explains the bad grades by such comments as "does not use time wisely," "homework incomplete," "not working to ability," "does not follow instructions."

Many of these young persons have outgrown their hyperactivity, have developed adequate motor control, or have made compensation for other handicaps. However, because these deficiencies prevented their acquiring the step-by-step learning as it was presented, they still lack the background needed to handle the upper-level tasks. They are now ready to learn the elementary skills, but teachers assume that all children at this level have mastered the basics and so do not teach them.

2. In addition to considering the inherent deficiency, a second factor affects the planning of a successful program.

The characteristics seen now as misbehavior, immaturity, or emotional disturbance are to be expected if a student has gone through six or more years of school but achieved little success and no recognition of the cause of his problems. A psychologist stated, "They would not be normal if they weren't reacting."

Many are so disturbed about their situation or the disabilities that have so affected normal functioning that they may be permanently scarred, and psychotherapy will be required. And yet, there is little use in trying to convince a youth that he is of worth to himself and society when daily he is being told that he isn't trying, that he's lazy, and seeing his efforts rejected for reasons he cannot help or understand.

Even the normal adolescent is vulnerable to the pressures of school, the change from elementary to secondary level. The student with learning handicaps, not yet ready for all the changes and new demands, is subject to much greater stress.

Most of these troubled youth can succeed in school and remain healthy individuals if the behaviors are recognized as being the result of their disabilities rather than the cause.

A judge discovered that a seventeen-year-old youth who was before the court on a first offense could not read. In sentencing him to a rehabilitation center to learn, the judge said, "Isn't it a shame? I kind of think he's been cheated out of an education."

3. The handicaps must not prevent learning.

As with younger children, one of the major obstacles in the path of disabled adolescents is the inability to master the taking of tests and the completion of assignments. Either they cannot read the material, cannot write the answers, are unable to think of the exact word needed, or the excessive tension of test-taking and timed responses proves to be too much.

Other methods of evaluation must be used so that their efforts are given recognition and no further damage done to their self-concept.

A senior-high student had made straight Fs in agriculture. In contacting the teacher, the father was told, "Oh, yes, Jim is one of my best students in class participation. He knows what we are talking about."

"Then why does he continue to make such bad grades?" the father queried. "He needs that credit to graduate."

"It's the tests. He never passes one, and you know that's what I have to grade on," said the teacher emphatically.

Another teacher told a parent that her son who was failing understood the stories they read in literature class as well as anyone. "Sometimes," she said, "he's the only one who gets the author's meaning. If he could only do better in his written work," she sighed resignedly.

Other students, because of lack of organization or poor auditory functioning so that they seldom "hear" assignments, seem never to do homework or finish booklets or get other details completed on time. They then make bad grades even though they have scored well on exams.

Thus, grades determine success or failure but may not indicate whether the student is learning. One teacher solved her problem by marking a student's paper A/F with the comment, "You have a wealth of information but also a wealth of grammatical errors."

In addition to different methods of evaluation needed to determine achievement, a major obstacle faces the brighter student—placement in classes based on test scores and grades.

Most learning-disabled students are assigned to basic or no-better-than-average classes. Often they are made to repeat the same things many times, some of which they understood long ago but are not allowed to prove in their way that they know it. Or, it is being taught in a way unsuitable to them and they cannot learn it.

Gary could not pass trigonometry in high school even after two tries. In junior college, however, he served as part-time instructor for the math classes because he already knew everything they were studying. He had known it earlier but could not perform in the way required by the individual instructor.

Aaron, with an IQ of over 140, was kept in a basic math class through seventh, eighth, and ninth grades because he was slow, unorganized, made frequent erasures, and did not listen well—the remnants of learning disabilities which were considered remediated in the early grades. Now, in high school, he is not ready for the more advanced courses that he needs in his pursuit of becoming a doctor.

Tim in the eighth grade had a paper route and kept records in his head. He was good at many things outside of school. His Stanford Achievement Test stanines were all in the lowest range possible, and he was placed in below average (and to him very boring) classes. His explanation for such low scores which do not reflect his ability was, "I can never finish in time. And I have trouble putting the answer in the right place for that computer to grade."

The gifted students, many of whom have or had learning handicaps are apt to learn and perform differently from other students. They need to have their potential emphasized and to not be held back by scores, grades, and class placement unsuitable for them. Some could be placed in a lower class in one subject and advanced in others.

A student said facetiously, "I can't pass anyway. At least I could fail in an interesting class."

A disability may prevent them from performing as some students, and they may not make any better grades no matter where they are. But their gifted mentalities enable them to learn in spite of handicaps if they are challenged and interested.

Since there are few special teachers available beyond the elementary level, someone must serve as an advocate, the friend indeed, for these exceptional teen-agers. The guidance counselor may not be the one because of lack of time or training.

This individual advocate, providing still the needed "watch care," will counsel with the student, institute new programs, and communicate with other teachers and parents concerning him. The attitude must be one of "we've got a problem," not just "you," lest the young person be made to feel that everything that is wrong is his fault.

Many of the adjustments listed in chapter 6 apply to the older student as well as the appropriateness of tactile and kinesthetic learning described in chapter 5.

In addition—

allow pupils to tutor younger children who are working on the needed skill;

establish a buddy system, someone to type class notes, to read aloud;

encourage use of a tape recorder and other audio-visuals as well as oral exams;

teach math through games and concrete experiences, and reading with newspapers, magazines, and popular songs;

recognize the teen's potential and interests, and take into account his aspirations and values.

College or Vocational Training?

The many stories of successful people who were hampered by learning problems obviously indicate that college is not only a possibility but a necessity for some students who perform inadequately in school.

There are several explanations for this contradiction. One is the basic, even brilliant intelligence of some which enables them to make their way and achieve whatever they want to even while seeming to fail.

A pediatrician who was a very poor reader said teasingly, "Well, I got married so I would have someone to read to me. Seriously," he continued, "nearly everything is on tape. And I wanted to be a doctor. Anyone can do it if they are willing to work hard."

Another reason is the continued maturation of adolescents into early adulthood. They tend to outgrow or make adjustments for their deficiencies. A student in college expressed his own puzzlement, "I've just discovered that math could be fun. I never understood a word of it all through regular school."

Still many do not want to, or should not, go to college. For them a vocational or prevocational track is to be preferred.

96

However, they often run into the same difficulties if a great deal of reading or conformity is required there also.

Many learning-disabled students need to be put into alternate programs as early as eighth grade, but rarely is anything available so soon.

Parents and advocates for these youth may have to press for modified requirements that fit the needs of the individual pupil. Rules can be changed so that the student does not suffer through some program designed for the average one or drop out because he cannot tolerate the pressure any longer.

These young people should not be sold short. Their natural abilities and fighting spirits (else they would not be in school still) allow them to go to college and to realize their aspirations.

Now some colleges are taking all this into account and are waiving entrance requirements and providing alternate programs. Parents may contact the national ACLD for a listing of such schools.

The Influence of Home

At a time when most adolescents are developing independence, the youth with learning disabilities has more than the normal need for parental support and guidance. The guidance may lie primarily in allowing them to "do their own thing" and to support principally the strong belief that they will become happy and independent adults.

Because such young persons mature later and may approach things differently, parents tend to concentrate on the worrisome characteristics and are concerned too much about the future.

How an adult helps the troubled youth becomes of utmost importance. This is an emotional age, one of resentments and uncertainties. There can be no behind-the-scenes management.

This comes about in several ways.

"How can I help?" is the attitude to be preferred rather than threats or demands.

Harry had to pass the course in driver's education before he could get a license. In answer to his parents' offer to help, he said, "If someone would read the book to me, I think I could learn it."

For hours at a time each night for several weeks, his mother and father took turns reading to him. Harry passed the course.

With an accepting attitude surrounding him and an uncritical person available, a teen-ager can feel free to ask for advice and assistance. A girl may admit her lack of social graces and ask an older family member to teach her to dance or how to wear makeup. She may even ask someone to talk to a teacher if she feels that she will be represented as desired.

Another way parents nurture is by providing opportunity to explore a variety of experiences so that the youngster may choose what interests him. There is need to recognize these abilities as pivotal points in the youth's future. Success in school may never be achieved, but a teen-ager may find satisfaction in pottery-making, a music group, or scuba diving.

Mental health centers offer group-therapy sessions that are beneficial to a troubled person who needs to talk things out with others having similar experiences.

Adults in the home also help by accepting the situation for what it is, admitting that there are deficiencies, that mistakes were made, that there are no easy solutions. The ignore-it-and-maybe-it-will-go-away approach will not work nor will pity or coddling the young person.

It is helpful for a child or adult to know that these mistakes and misunderstandings are rooted in handicaps that still are not understood nor recognized adequately but which are the fault òf no one.

Maintaining a strong belief in the future of the adolescent enables him to have hope. If a parent gives up or reacts angrily, so will the youth.

Parents may need to take courses in parenting or to participate in group counseling sessions in order to get a better perspective.

Adolescents with learning handicaps cannot be compared with their brothers and sisters or with others of the same age. One cannot be the model teen-ager in looks or actions.

An understanding teacher once said that a child who can't spell *anxiety* can tell you what it means. "Rather than marking off for spelling," he said, "it is better to listen to what he has to say."

The following poem was written by a high-school student who could not spell or punctuate and who barely made passing grades.

I Am I–You Are You

> *You like short hair.*
> *You like soft music.*

99

You like certain things politically.
You like walls with nothing on them.
You like things very orderly.
You like small calendars.
You like all of this and this is how
    you function best;
And with all of this and more
You are you
And I am proud of that.
    But
I like long hair.
I like loud music.
I like certain things politically.
I like posters on my walls.
I like my calendars big.
I like all of this and this is how
    I function best;
And with all of this and more
I am I
And I am proud of that also.
Obviously there is conflict.
Obviously we cannot live by the same standards.

For you are you
And I am I
    But
I don't ask you to grow your hair.
And I don't ask you to put posters
    on your walls.
And I don't ask that you only express
    those beliefs parallel with mine.
And I don't ask you to play your music loud.

And whether or not we understand each other,
We are still different even if one of us

THE ADOLESCENT

Makes no sense at all to the other one.
You are still you and I am still I.

I am not a child anymore.
And I have got to be I
Just as much as
You have got to be you.

CHAPTER VIII

The Learning-Disabled Child at Church

Children and youth who have not found success in school often are failures at church also.

Most are children who have been scarred by their experiences and are unsure of themselves; some are unable to sit still here either; others refuse to participate in school-like activities. These are the overly bright ones who are bored and the slower ones who need extra challenges. Often their difficulties are labeled simply behavior problems and it is said that "someone ought to do something."

Forced to attend a certain number of years of school, they do not have to attend church activities. If they are not made to feel comfortable here and their needs met, they become the dropouts who are listed as the ones needing visiting, the juvenile delinquents who are discussed in well-planned programs or the mentally ill about whom such sympathy is expressed.

The church, a community of the concerned, should be able to encompass all types of personality and needs. Often that is not the case. A Sunday school teacher was heard to say, "He's just a troublemaker. I wish he would quit coming."

Sometimes children are seen sitting outside the classroom in the hallway in isolation. Others will not attend for fear of having to read aloud or to sit quietly for so long. Some youth groups seem to exclude those who do not conform to their ways of learning or manner of dress.

They have been cast out, their potential unnoticed, their needs unmet, their cares unshared.

People are still as they have always been. Joseph in the Old Testament evidently was not easy to get along with. His brothers hated his boasting, so they got rid of him. In a new land and under adversity, he became a leader.

The disciples must have been difficult for Jesus to teach. They often misunderstood and tried to intervene in what he was doing. They went to sleep, ran away, and some denied him. But Jesus was patient and showed confidence in them, and they became the leaders of a new order.

So it can be today and children and young people should not be discouraged from participating until they can be as others think they should be. Neither should they be condemned for being as they are.

Pointing to a crippled man, someone asked Jesus, "Who sinned, this man or his parents?" Jesus answered, "No one has sinned. His condition is not the fault of him or his parents."

These children are so because of their own growth patterns and the inappropriate demands placed upon them by society.

Parents desperately seek aid from the church to help meet the challenges posed by their offspring but often are met only with criticism.

The church must be a healing force involved in reaching out to everyone, even those who are very difficult to reach, not only to someone who conforms and presents few challenges.

Perhaps the story of this little boy could be the story of a child in Jesus' time.

Joel couldn't sit still in the synagogue classes. He didn't understand much of what was going on so he pinched the boys sitting so close to him on the floor. He couldn't seem to keep his feet under him when they sat in neat rows on their mats.

Joel's parents forced him to attend the school, and he hated it. Once when no one was looking, he unrolled one of the sacred scrolls and left it open on the floor.

Of course, everyone knew who had done this terrible deed. It was the final offense. Joel was forbidden to attend anymore, but he didn't tell his parents.

One day Jesus came by the small building and saw Joel sitting dejectedly outside. He stopped to talk even though the men with him urged him on.

Joel found himself telling Jesus how everyone wants him to be quiet, to be still, how no one listens to him. Jesus listened.

So when Jesus and the other men went on, Joel gathered up his lunch and his wrap and trailed along behind. He followed them to a hillside where many people assembled to hear Jesus teach. He was so interested that he stayed and stayed.

After a while people were saying that they were hungry, but there was nothing to eat.

Joel remembered his small lunch with the fish and bread. He ran to Jesus with it and said, "It isn't much but I want you to have it."

How Can Their Needs Be Met?

1. By experiential teaching. The abstract ideas of religion have to be couched in actual or simulated experiences in order to be understood and remembered.

Little of what is heard is remembered, more of what is seen

and heard, but most of what is experienced is retained. Therefore, much teaching is lost because it is not done in the manner that is learned best.

The story of the good Samaritan will be long remembered if a few costumes are added to active young boys and girls, and they are urged to act it out.

"Shepherd, shepherd, where are you going?" questions one group of small children using the words of their song. While the rest in costume answer walking as they sing, "Down to the stable where the baby's born."

Youth groups can do interviews, role-play, commune with God through nature rather than just talking or reading about these things.

As one studies the Bible it can be readily seen that Jesus taught in many different ways—through stories and parables, as he healed and performed miracles, while they walked and ate and lived together. He used real-life situations—the sparrow's falling from the sky, the fish that must have been eaten daily, the washing of their feet.

The scribes and pharisees said that one must wear special clothes and worship only in customary ways, but Jesus said that much of what they did was hypocritical. He said the needs of the individual are what count, not the customs and laws, as he healed on the sabbath and allowed his disciples to pluck grain.

This is still true today, and the willingness to incorporate many ways of learning will largely determine whether children enjoy and want to attend church activities.

A teacher attending a workshop explained her reasons for not using any of the ideas presented saying, "We don't need them. We go around the circle reading the lesson. They like it that way.'' Someone in the back of the room muttered, ''The ones who still come, you mean.''

Students who do not like to read or do not learn best that way or cannot sit still are thus cast out.

Of course, the most effective teaching of all is done by the way the adults act and feel toward the ones being taught, more that way than by what is said.

2. Encourage their talents and interests and utilize these in meaningful ways.

Some children like to be ''up front'' talking and leading, others prefer to make costumes and paint sets, to make collages. Some like to read aloud and can read as needed, others would rather create something to illustrate the idea. Many enjoy just being part of a group that accepts them as they are.

However, there are times when a child cannot be handled in a regular class or a teen-ager is not comfortable with his own age group, but they need not be isolated. An extra volunteer (not the parents—they need the time apart) can be assigned to help the child through some of the activities. An older youngster can be allowed to help with the younger children.

Attendance at the regularly scheduled activities may not be possible, but there are many things that can be done at other times to help the young person think of church as a happy place.

Reece hated Sunday school and did not participate in the youth-group activities, but he wired a sound system into the social hall and was called frequently to set up lighting arrangements and to fix broken wires. He felt and was part of the church.

Church dinners were the favorite times for David because he was allowed to help run the dishwasher. Soon he was being paid to wash the dishes for many of the larger functions; he volunteered many hours also. He felt that the kitchen was his special place in the church.

Wanda loved small children. The young parents knew this and preferred that she keep the nursery whenever possible. Wanda felt that she was helping her church.

Any child can be taught to be an acolyte or to rearrange hymnbooks, to help grow a garden, or be allowed to use imagination in painting the youth room or keeping the grounds in order.

The church can provide dedicated leaders who share their values and talents in music and craft classes, photography and art, recreation, and whatever else is available through the members.

A person needs to feel uniquely valuable, especially at church. There, a belief in oneself can be reaffirmed even though one may feel the rest of the world to be hostile.

3. Special Considerations.

Placement. Even though a child fails a year of school, he need not lose a year of his whole life. It may be best to allow him to remain with his age group at church.

Attendance at Worship Services. A child who does not like formal services may not understand what is happening. An adult should go over the services with him ahead of time and teach the responses. Some children do not catch onto the way the words follow along in the hymns.

A child who cannot sit still may need something to do with his hands. Materials and directions for drawing the minister, the choir, the setting help center attention on what is happening.

A father explained his success, "For years I used to draw on Raymond's hand during the sermon. It seemed to release excess energy, and we both could listen."

Music and Choir. There are many ways that a child can benefit and enjoy music participation. He does not have to be especially skilled and may even be tone deaf.

Children who learn to play instruments should be encouraged to use this skill within the program of the church.

The psalms frequently mention praising God with music—cymbals and lyre, for example. Rhythm instruments played along with the reading of one of these help make the meaning clearer. See Psalms 98; 68:25.

"The Atypical Child in Choir" by Christine Kallstrom (see Resources) is an excellent guide for ways a choir director can help children with learning disabilities. She says, "The Bible is filled with examples of therapeutic uses of music—and those of us who would truly minister with music have an obligation to use our gift to help all children who come to us become more 'whole' through the healing powers of our art form."

4. The church can participate along with others in the community in recognizing the needs of these children and youth and can help provide solutions for the problems, not only at church but elsewhere:

—by presenting programs at the various meetings within the church, including the youth, and discussing their characteristics at teacher planning and training sessions (see film *Walk in Another Pair of Shoes*). Background information on the neurological and emotional development should be presented along with an attempt to change the attitude from one of "If he or she would only—" to one of how to change the atmosphere within the church so that they can be comfortable, secure, and can participate satisfactorily. They do not need to have special groups established for them.

—by providing parent counseling-groups and pastoral care by someone who has learned about these things and can at least communicate about the problems.

—by encouraging the formation of local ACLD and allowing the meetings to be held at the church.

—by providing facilities and volunteers for after-school or Saturday tutoring and developmental programs and summer day camps.

—by including developmental training within the nursery and kindergarten day classes held at the church. Observant teachers can spot atypical children or just troublesome characteristics in some and give a little extra care in helping them.

Much is learned from children who have difficulties. It has been said that education will be greatly changed from the application of what has been recently discovered about learning disabilities. The same is true within the church. The children who create the trying situations often become the leaders if they are not rejected.

Jesus said to his disciples, "Let the children come. Don't forbid them." The church must not reject or forbid even the loudest or the quietest, the most cooperative or the balky ones, the easy to teach nor the ones who need extra time and patience.

Where else can they find acceptance if not within the fellowship of the church?

CHAPTER IX

In the Community

The activities of the community should round out the life of a young person, providing avenues of growth and new opportunities for learning. For a youth or child with learning disabilities these can be as important as the formal education a child is receiving if he is unhappy and is not learning as expected.

Few of these children, however, can find their own activities. They are too aggressive and so are shunned; they are not equipped to play as the other children do, and they fail; or they are too shy and unskilled to make proper advances.

Randy had looked forward to becoming a Cub Scout. He was proud of the new uniform and had gone eagerly to meetings. Suddenly he did not want to go anymore.

His father was troubled. He called Mrs. Forrest, the leader, to apologize. Mrs. Forrest unknowingly explained the difficulty when she said, ''Oh, yes, we're still waiting for Randy to say the oath in front of the group. He hasn't learned it yet.''

Randy has a memory problem and is frightened to stand before a group, even a small one. He might forget, and they would laugh as others have.

Mona sits in her room or grouses throughout the house most of the time. She has few friends even though several neighbor girls have tried in the past to get her out to play. They finally gave up.

110

Troy is the neighborhood terror and is forbidden to enter the yards of the houses nearby. Most of the owners don't speak to his mother, either.

Parents of these and other children have to give more than the usual amount of guidance in making sure that their son or daughter knows how to participate. Also much time will have to be spent helping the adults of the community understand so that the child is not made an outcast.

Scouting, Camp Fire Girls

Children with learning disabilities, most of whom belong in regular units, are often rejected because they do not behave in meetings or on camping trips, are unable to complete many of the requirements, or do not become completely involved because they need extra help which may not be available.

A once-eager young Scout convinced his parents to let him quit. Later he explained, "I never caught on to what they were doing. Everyone seemed to know but me," he said sadly.

Someone must take the time to give further explanation to those who need it. Many do not absorb the instructions, perhaps given in a jumble of noise. Others need assistance in understanding badge or advancement rquirements, in remembering the time or place of planned activities, and additional practice for upcoming requirements such as fire-building and cooking for a camp-out.

A hand on the shoulder for the talkative ones is better than being required to write essays, as one Camp Fire leader does when her girls are not quiet. Many cannot just sit and listen for long periods of time, particularly after a worrisome day at school.

If a child cannot read, arrangements must be made to see that he gets the information some other way; those who do not listen or do not remember what they hear need to have it printed.

A suggestion of keeping a notebook is helpful as a reminder. A verification by an adult or a call to the parent may be necessary to see if the child has heard correctly.

Many children need help with crafts or other requirements that utilize manual dexterity, because they have handicaps that interfere with the completion of a satisfactory project. Recognition must be given for effort and not just the end product.

While most of the cooperation is spurred by parent interest, many seem not to be concerned. Their children may need more help.

The creed of the majority of these groups involves service and helpfulness. Those who are skilled and successful can be helped to carry out their promises by being taught concern for others not so fortunate within their own ranks.

Sports and Recreation

Competitive team sports such as Little League may be suitable for some children, but many are not able to handle the pressures or are not skilled enough to attempt the fine precision needed to be successful.

Other provisions have to be made so that sports and recreational activities are not omitted from a child's life, no matter how clumsy he may be. Many ACLD chapters have organized Saturday classes for developmental exercises. Boy's Clubs provide a variety of activities that emphasize evaluation of one's own development and achievements.

Perhaps the organized teams of a community could be persuaded to provide for such training as may be necessary and for supervised, but noncompetitive, play. Unsportsmanlike behavior improves with careful teaching rather than punishment.

A youth may find surprising interest and talent in an unfamiliar sport if exposed to it. So he should be given the opportunity to try many different ones—karate, archery, wrestling, weight lifting, and so on.

The lack of good motor skills or long endurance should not be misread to mean that a person does not care about sports. Everyone can and should find something enjoyable and that can be done to the person's satisfaction.

Camp

Camping can be one of the most beneficial of all experiences, but for many children their first contact is traumatic. Others are afraid to try it and thus miss out on one of the joys of growing up.

There is need for caution, however. A child should not be sent to camp without adequate preparation on his part as well as the staff of the camp. The same troublesome attributes cause children to be isolated and punished, harassed, and made fun of.

Activities that prepare for camping should be experienced

gradually, starting with day camp, then a one- or two-night exposure. Of course, the child will have spent nights away from home previously.

There are camps especially suited to children with learning and motor handicaps. These are often established by individual chapters of ACLD. A group of concerned parents can initiate such a camp. Church camps usually are willing to make adjustments as necessary.

Most learning-disabled children can participate in regular camps where the staff has been alerted to their needs. A child may also attend summer school while at camp, for there are some that include educational programming as well as the usual activities.

The national office of ACLD and Closer Look provide a list of camps. Check Resources for further information.

Music Lessons

A well-known singer told in an interview that she could not read music. Yet, she sang, played the piano, and wrote her own songs. "A lot of musicians do not read music," she explained.

Many children gifted with abundant musical talent find lessons unbearable. Some are able to pursue their interests in spite of this. Others give up. Even those not so talented can learn to their satisfaction if thought is given to teaching them in many different ways. Their handicaps must be considered but should not prevent progress.

The same principal applies here as elsewhere—allow the

child to learn through his strength while practicing and working to improve the weak areas.

For example: if the student learns best by an aural method but does not sight-read well enough to keep up interest, use an approach that emphasizes the auditory modality.

If visual learning is slowed by—

1) inability to find the place or keep the sight focused on the line, then use a line marker or a keyhole marker so that only the note or section desired is seen;

2) not proceeding from left to right, use a star on the starting point with arrows indicating the direction the eyes should move;

3) difficulty separating main figure from the background, use color cues and outline the notes or the lines with a felt marker;

4) poor memory, then teach kinesthetically. Trace symbols in the air or on raised material while looking at them and saying them. Repeat without looking. Outline whole and half notes with yarn or pipestem cleaners and fill in quarter notes or less with felt so that the child can feel the difference. Refresh memory this way before attempting to play.

If a child displays inadequate reading skills, find out if possible what the diagnosis is, and use this information to plan the correct approach. Otherwise, do not require a great deal of reading in order to learn to play.

When auditory functioning seems below normal, emphasis will have to be upon visual learning with corrective emphasis in the auditory channel.

The differences in pitch, rhythms, tones, and so forth, will have to be overemphasized, perhaps with exercises other than

115

at the instrument. Responding physically to rhythm and mood adds to learning.

The teacher will have to be careful how fast and how much he talks as well as of the pitch of the voice. No talking at all is sometimes necessary. Assignments must be written.

The degree of motor control affects skill in playing. As a child expressed it, "I've got it in my head, but I can't get it into my hands." Additional exercises then could include squeezing a rubber ball or practicing commands from the eye or ear to the hands.

Place a design on the left hand with a similar marking near notes played by that hand. A left-handed pupil is not hampered, but one whose dominance is not established probably will be. This applies even to a teen-ager.

The playing must be done correctly the first time so that incorrect responses are not learned. The proper motor patterns can be taught apart from the instrument.

1. Memory: If a child seems unable to play without looking at the music, this should not slow him down. He may never be able to memorize but can play skillfully.

2. Hyperactivity: Long periods of concentration usually are not possible, but a variety of related activities can be included in each session. Sometimes the pace if quickened, even though technique is not acquired as thoroughly as might be desired, keeps the student interested.

3. Erratic behavior: This is typical of learning-disabled children both emotionally as well as physically. Most benefit from a minimum of emphasis upon the mistakes.

4. Overloading: Sometimes a child seems to be unable to receive or express himself visually, auditorily, and kinesthetically at the same time. He may either figuratively or actually

close his eyes or ears against too much stimulation, or his coordination may be affected. He may need quiet time to think and plan the next move.

How music is organized in the brain is not well understood. Each person, however, has his unique way of acquiring the knowledge and skill, and the instruction must be geared to how the pupil learns, not to how the teacher likes best to teach.

Music can be a soothing force in a troubled person's life. It can be the succès d'estime for someone who has known only failure.

Other Community Resources

The child who does not learn by the normal and expected means should be given the opportunity to learn through a variety of exposures. He will experience things that will be absorbed and utilized more than can be measured.

These resources include fabric shops, animal shows, botanical gardens, exhibits of every kind—mineral, art craft—factories, farms, zoos, the library, ice cream plants, and many others.

The usual tourist attractions may prove to be unduly exciting. Most visits, even to the grocery store, have to be short and well-structured.

The Neighborhood

Outside the home: Children who have a low opinion of themselves are more apt to cause or be trouble in the unstructured atmosphere of the neighborhood.

117

One may be labeled a bully and perhaps blamed for everything that goes wrong, or the children of the neighborhood "pick on" a susceptible child. Or worse, there may be no contact at all, the child hesitant or afraid to venture out.

A young person who is unhappy may take out his frustrations on animals or people. He may lie, steal, be destructive, or use bad language. Punishment rarely improves the behavior. Understanding why the child acts that way and engaging the aid of a few others will be more helpful.

This means that parents will have to plan carefully where and what their children play, how long, and with whom. This applies to an older child as well.

Neighbors can be abusive to parents as well as children and some of them have to be avoided. Others can be enlisted to help if time is taken to let them know about the worries and heartaches of being learning disabled. They, then, might be willing to invite such a child into their homes to bake cookies, share a hobby, or even to sit on the steps and talk.

A teen-ager or surrogate grandparent could be hired occasionally to "watch over," teach a craft, or just play with one or several children who need supervision but also need some freedom away from their own yard.

Inside the home: The need for continued planning never ends in that it involves those who come into the home. These include playmates, baby-sitters, and even relatives.

The insecure child who does not know how to go out and play must first have companions brought in—one, then a few at a time—under careful supervision. Even with a young adolescent, this is sometimes necessary.

Birthday parties prove troublesome for hyperactive children or ones who are not at ease in a crowd. Too many people, too much excitement, or the wrong kind of games do not contribute to a happy occasion. Making a cake with a friend or two, a treasure or scavenger hunt for only a few persons, a mystery trip, or a friend to spend the night may be more satisfying.

Baby-sitters especially have to be chosen carefully. They must always understand the fears and expected behaviors—however difficult—as well as what gives pleasure to the child.

Four-year-old Alton was diagnosed as having an auditory perception problem. He used substitute words in speaking. The parents were told to hand him what he wanted as they repeated the correct word but to use no punitive measures. The baby-sitter did not agree and frequently told the parents that if they would quit talking for him, he would learn to speak correctly.

Once upon return of the parents, an older brother reported that the sitter had caused Alton to cry for several hours because she would not give him the milk when he said "ba," even though she knew what he wanted.

She was not hired again.

Some teen-agers, especially, are good with young children, but others know only how to threaten and punish to get their way.

Great harm can be done to an already damaged ego by allowing persons who are not prepared, to care for such a child. The right person adds much pleasure and new dimension to a child's life and gives the parents much needed respite.

Relatives, also, must be offered information. If the time spent with them is not satisfactory, it must be limited.

However, a few suggestions to the adult may increase the pleasure.

Parents must not feel guilty in doing what they feel is best if they have sought professional advice, even though there be those within the family who disagree.

CHAPTER X

Action and Resources

The international Association for Children with Learning Disabilities, only a few more than ten years old, is now one of the largest service organizations in the world. Rarely has an organization grown so fast.

Parents and professionals from all the disciplines have cooperated in forming a viable group which has effected legislation, instituted new programs and procedures, and received community support and understanding for this more lately recognized but largest group of handicapped children.

There may be many agencies in the community and departments within the school system that have been made aware of the plight of these children and are providing some services. Rarely do any of these become involved in the total life of the child and provide services for the parents as well.

ACLD was formed for this purpose—to be a unifying agent in the community and to create services not already available.

Most of the efforts to organize ACLD are initiated by concerned parents but many pediatricians, eye doctors, psychologists, and teachers are ready to participate in an effort to effect change. Many of the professionals have been frustrated because so many children come to them for help, and there is much more that needs to be done than they can do individually for the child.

By writing the national ACLD, interested individuals can secure information about how to begin a local chapter. Usually a few parents, several interested professionals, and representatives of related agencies in the community as well as representatives from the public school system are the nucleus.

The school officials must be included at the very beginning, for no effort is complete without an adequate educational approach. There is usually someone who is knowledgeable and interested who is willing to help. However, elected school board members, a superintendent, and director of special education should be included as well. They make the decisions on new programs and finances. Their support and knowlege of these children are vital.

The literature of the association stresses the importance of preschool screening, in-service training for teachers, the training and use of volunteer tutors. Also emphasized are the rights of parents concerning an adequate education for handicapped children and the privilege of being told information that has been gathered about their children.

In addition to more adequate school programs, the need for political action is stressed in order to have more funds available. Affiliation with national and state associations is urged so that a greater impact is made.

Also local chapters have to concern themselves with the need for preschool preventive programs, recreational activities, out-of-school tutoring, parent counseling groups, and, most of all, public awareness.

Many other service clubs have adopted learning disabilities as their major concern. Through their ''Younger Years Project,'' 1974–75, the Kiwanis International has provided thousands of dollars in aid as did the General Federation of Women's Clubs, Junior, 1974–76.

In one community the Junior League provided a large

financial grant, and with the cooperation of Kiwanis and other service clubs and under the guidance of the ACLD a new Resource Center was established. This center, with a unique liaison with the public school system, provides services, including tutoring, but serves mainly as a co-ordinating and referral agency.

In another community a Kiwanis Club funded a new diagnostic center. Often the United Fund and March of Dimes make grants available.

Parents no longer need feel that they are not being heard. Much has been done and they can do more. Through support of others who are also affected, they can maintain self-respect when uninformed persons say that it is their fault that their children behave and learn as they do. They can help establish avenues to improve their own skills and be a catalyst for improving the lot of others.

Resources

Agencies

1. Association for Children with Learning Disabilities (ACLD), 5221 Grace Street, Lower Level, Pittsburg, PA 15236.

   ACLD Newsbriefs is published monthly—$1.00 per year. A national convention is held annually, and many states sponsor yearly conferences. Also published is a list of recommended books and films available for sale and rent through the national office.

2. Closer Look, Box 1492, Washington, DC 20013.

   Closer Look is a national information center, a project of the U.S. Department of Health, Education and Welfare, Office of Education, Bureau of Education for the

Handicapped. It directs parents to the closest resource for information about the rights of parents, tax laws that allow tutoring and other expenses to be deducted, camps for the handicapped, et cetera. It also publishes a quarterly *Report from Closer Look* which helps to keep information current.

3. The National Easter Seal Society for Crippled Children and Adults, 2023 West Ogden Avenue, Chicago, IL 60612.
   The Society publishes an excellent selective listing of literature available on the brain-injured child and informs where to order. Many publications are available at minimal cost from the Society. Learning disabilities is one of the handicaps for which services are provided through Easter Seal centers. A list of such centers can be secured from the national office.

4. U.S. Department of Health, Education and Welfare (HEW), Division of Handicapped Children and Youth, U.S. Office of Education, Washington, DC 20202.
   In addition to determining priorities and administering funds, this department participates actively in research and helps assess the needs of the present and future of handicapped children.

   Of interest to those persons involved with learning disabilities are three publications which resulted from joint study of committees composed of representatives from the National Institute of Neurological Diseases and Blindness of HEW, the Easter Seal Research Foundation, other departments within the U.S. Office of Education, and many other public and volunteer agencies, including ACLD. These publications highlight the research findings as well as the prominent persons in the field.

The publications may be ordered from the Superintendent of Documents, U.S. Government Printing Office, Washington, DC 20402, or from the National Easter Seal Society for $.30.

The publications are:

Minimal Brain Dysfunction in Children: Terminology and Identification, Phase One. Public Health Services, Publ. no. 1415. $1.00.

Minimal Brain Dysfunction in Children: Educational, Medical and Health Related Services, Phase Two. Public Health Services, Publ. no. 2015. $1.00.

Central Processing Dysfunction in Children: A Review of Research, Phase Three, Monograph no. 9. $1.25.

5. The Talking Book Service, Division for the Blind and Physically Handicapped, Library of Congress, Washington, DC 20542.

   This service is available to persons who are unable to read because of disabilities or other limitations. The service includes free earphones, record players, and "talking books" for all ages. Some regional libraries provide the materials.

Films

1. *Introduction to Learning Disabilities.* 30 min. Color. Excellent for parents and teachers.

   Public Health Service, National Institute of Health, National Medical Audiovisual Center Annex, Station K, Atlanta, GA 30324.

2. *They Can Learn.* 15 min. Color. For parents and teachers. Real Time, 529 North Columbus Street, Alexandria, VA 22314.

3. *Walk in Another Pair of Shoes.* 18 min. Color slides.

Accompanied by cassette tape of narration by Ernie Ford. Suitable to show to older children as well as adults. Minimum fee.

CANHC Movie Distribution. P. O. Box 4088, Los Angeles, CA 90051.

Adolescent:

4. *If a Boy Can't Learn*. 25 min. Color.

Suitable for parents and professionals. Preview fee $10.00. Lawren Productions, P. O. Box 1542, Burlingame, CA 94010.

5. *Adolescence and Learning Disabilities*. 25 min. Color.

Designed to accompany the above film but aimed principally at teachers and professionals. Order from the same address.

6. *Youth in Trouble*. Videotapes of a symposium by the same name. Write for more information to: Texas ACLD, 7986 Fallmeadow Lane, Dallas, TX 75240.

Publications

Adolescent:

1. An excellent list of recommended books and how to order each is available from the California Association for Neurologically Handicapped Children (CANHC), Literature Distribution Center, P. O. Box 1526, Vista, CA 92083.

CANHC also publishes or has available books and articles on every topic about learning disabilities in addition to films, games, and a monthly newsletter.

2. Academic Therapy Publications, 1543 Fifth Avenue, San Rafael, CA 94901.

This company is the largest publisher of books exclusively on the various topics in the field of learning disabilities. It also publishes a quarterly journal entitled *Academic Therapy* for lay and professional persons. Single copy $2.00; yearly subscription $6.00.

3. *Journal of Learning Disabilities*, 5 North Wabash Avenue, Chicago IL 60602.

   For educators. Publishes 10 issues yearly. Single copy $1.50; subscription $10.00.

   Writing:

4. The Jean Riley Publishing Company, 415 North East Street, Arlington, TX 76012.

   This new nonprofit corporation has been established to maintain and operate facilities for the printing, publication, and distribution of written or transcribed material contributed by disabled individuals who will be paid for the work accepted. This applies to persons who have learning disabilities severe enough to qualify them as being disabled.

5. *I Can Do*. A handwriting series for children with special needs.

   Write for list of materials to: Zaner-Bloser, 612 North Park Street, Columbus, OH 43215.

   Pencil Grippers. Order from MKM, 809 Kansas City Street, Rapid City, SD 57701. Eight for $1.00; 100 for $9.00.

6. *The Left Hand Catalogue*, 140 West 22nd Street, New York, NY 10011. Enclose $1.00 which can be applied to purchase.

   Music:

7. "The Atypical Child in Choir." Christine Kallstrom.

CANHC, Literature Distribution Center, P. O. Box 1526 Vista, CA 92083. $.15.

8. "Helping Learning Disabled Music Students." Dorothy Gilles and Valerie Kovitz. Cove School, 1100 Forest Avenue, Evanston, IL 60202. $.15.
Camps:

9. For information on how to set up a day camp for learning-disability children and other guidelines for camp activities, write to: Dorothy S. Dorion, 7922 Hunter's Grove Road, Jacksonville, FL 32216.
Arts and Crafts:

10. *A Word or Two About Learning Disabilities*. Doreen Kronick. Academic Therapy Publications. San Rafael, CA 94901, 1973.

11. *Recipes for Art and Craft Materials*. Helen Roney Sattler. New York: Lothrop, Lee and Shepard Co., 1973.

Additional Publications

1. *P.E.T.: Parent Effectiveness Training*. Dr. Thomas Gordon.
A book and parent training course.
P.E.T. Information, Effectiveness Training Associates, 110 South Euclid Avenue, Pasadena, CA 91101.

2. *The Misspeller's Dictionary*. Ed. by Peter and Craig Norback. Designed for people who spell the way they hear. New York; Quadrangle/The New York Times Book Co., New York, NY 10022, 1974.

3. *Dyslexia*. A paper on Reading Disabilities. Available free from the American Association of Ophthalmology. Check with a local doctor.

4. *A Parent's Guide to Minimal Brain Dysfunction, 1974*. CIBA Pharmaceutical Company, Summit, NJ.